Information Sciences Series

Editors

ROBERT M. HAYES
University of California
Los Angeles, California

JOSEPH BECKER
President
Becker and Hayes, Inc.

Consultant

CHARLES P. BOURNE
University of California
Berkeley, California

Joseph Becker and Robert M. Hayes:
INFORMATION STORAGE AND RETRIEVAL

Charles P. Bourne:
METHODS OF INFORMATION HANDLING

Harold Borko:
AUTOMATED LANGUAGE PROCESSING

Russell D. Archibald and Richard L. Villoria:
NETWORK-BASED MANAGEMENT SYSTEMS (PERT/CPM)

Launor F. Carter:
NATIONAL DOCUMENT-HANDLING SYSTEMS FOR SCIENCE AND TECHNOLOGY

Perry E. Rosove:
DEVELOPING COMPUTER-BASED INFORMATION SYSTEMS

F. W. Lancaster:
INFORMATION RETRIEVAL SYSTEMS

Ralph L. Bisco:
DATA BASES, COMPUTERS, AND THE SOCIAL SCIENCES

Charles T. Meadow
MAN-MACHINE COMMUNICATION

Gerald Jahoda:
INFORMATION STORAGE AND RETRIEVAL SYSTEMS FOR INDIVIDUAL RESEARCHERS

Robert M. Hayes and Joseph Becker:
HANDBOOK OF DATA PROCESSING FOR LIBRARIES

Allen Kent:
INFORMATION ANALYSIS AND RETRIEVAL

Robert S. Taylor:
THE MAKING OF A LIBRARY

Herman M. Weisman:
INFORMATION SYSTEMS, SERVICES, AND CENTERS

Jesse H. Shera:
THE FOUNDATIONS OF EDUCATION FOR LIBRARIANSHIP

Charles T. Meadow:
THE ANALYSIS OF INFORMATION SYSTEMS, Second Edition

Stanley J. Swihart and Beryl F. Hefley:
COMPUTER SYSTEMS IN THE LIBRARY

F. W. Lancaster and E. G. Fayen
INFORMATION RETRIEVAL ON-LINE

Richard A. Kaimann:
STRUCTURED INFORMATION FILES

Thelma Freides:
LITERATURE AND BIBLIOGRAPHY OF THE SOCIAL SCIENCES

Dagobert Soergel:
INDEXING LANGUAGES AND THESAURI: CONSTRUCTION AND MAINTENANCE

Structured Information Files

RICHARD A. KAIMANN
Marquette University
Milwaukee, Wisconsin

A Wiley-Becker & Hayes Series Book

 MELVILLE PUBLISHING COMPANY
Los Angeles, California

Copyright © 1973, by John Wiley & Sons, Inc.
Published by Melville Publishing Company,
a Division of John Wiley & Sons, Inc.

All rights reserved. Published simultaneously in Canada.

No part of this book may be reproduced by any means,
nor transmitted, nor translated into a machine language
without the written permission of the publisher.

Library of Congress Cataloging in Publication Data

Kaimann, Richard A
    Structured information files.

    (Information sciences series)
    Bibliography: p.
    1. Electronic digital computers—Programming.
2. Information storage and retrieval systems.
I. Title.

QA76.6.K34   029.7   73-8650
ISBN 0-471-45483-4

Printed in the United States of America

10 9 8 7 6 5 4 3 2 1

Information Sciences Series

Information is the essential ingredient in decision making. The need for improved information systems in recent years has been made critical by the steady growth in size and complexity of organizations and data.

This series is designed to include books that are concerned with various aspects of communicating, utilizing, and storing digital and graphic information. It will embrace a broad spectrum of topics, such as information system theory and design, man-machine relationships, language data processing, artificial intelligence, mechanization of library processes, nonnumerical applications of digital computers, storage and retrieval, automatic publishing, command and control, information display, and so on.

Information science may someday be a profession in its own right. The aim of this series is to bring together the interdisciplinary core of knowledge that is apt to form its foundation. Through this consolidation, it is expected that the series will grow to become the focal point for professional education in this field.

Preface

A reader of any reference or text should be concerned about where the book will take him. Hopefully, this preface will answer that question.

Computing has come a long way since the early 1950's when the computer was first introduced on the commercial scene. In the early 1960's, IBM introduced the mass market model 1401 (and later the 1410 and 1440). Both business data processing computer accounting departments and manufacturing departments adopted it. But the applications were different. Accounting was largely the task of processing transactions against a master file of data—time-consuming but relatively straightforward.

Manufacture and production required the storage of the component structure or bill of materials of each product as a data base. Requirements planning, shop routing, and dispatching could be performed from this base. These tasks required a data processing operation that could store and retrieve pieces of data in a disorganized, nonsequential fashion. It was termed *direct access* or *random access processing.*

Since many users were doing approximately the same data processing tasks, the vendors developed software packages as an aid and a marketing inducement. Thus by the time the IBM System 360 series was announced in 1964, these packages had reached a fairly sophisticated level.

These programs served a valuable function by eliminating the necessity of completely replicating programs with each user. But there was a negative effect. The design and development of random access files was slowed considerably. After all, why learn how to do it when all you had to do was learn how to use it.

With the 1970's, computing had reached a crisis. Companies claim they are not receiving a sufficient payoff from their computer investment. There are claims that the computer is idle 50% of the time. There are claims that the manufacturers oversold the product.

To appreciate these relationships, perhaps we should return to a basic understanding of computers. With a thorough grounding in basic concepts, the programmer and systems analyst will be in a position to increase the operating and use efficiency of the key commercial data processing systems and applications of the 1970's.

Therefore, this book on structured information files provides the basics in one aspect of computing. It focuses on how to design a random access file. Yet we do examine two key elements. First, how to get into the file or data base and, second, how to operate within the file to achieve the desired results.

ACKNOWLEDGEMENTS

Many thanks are due to many people. I offer my deepest gratitude to those people who worked with me and aided me at two universities. At the University of Iowa, there were Dr. Peter Schoderbek and Mr. Leon Pearce in the College of Business. Dr. Gerry Weeg and Mr. Paul Wolf in the University of Iowa Computer Center; and at Marquette University Dr. Lloyd Doney, and particularly, Dr. T. R. Martin, Dean of the College of Business Administration. Dr. Martin provided the time, resources, and often critical stimulation to push this work over the peak. The typing of this manuscript was done by Mrs. Gena Lindhorst at Iowa and Mrs. Dolores Rewolinski at Marquette. Without them the war, battle, horse, and shoe would have been lost.

Milwaukee, Wisconsin *Richard A. Kaimann*

Contents

One

Introduction   1

A.	Purpose of This Book	1
B.	The Need for Information	2
C.	Hardware Developments	5
D.	Unstructured Versus Structured Files	12
E.	Summary	15

Two

Background   16

A.	The Interdependence of Storage and Retrieval	16
B.	Random and Sequential Files	17
C.	Characterizing Stored Information	18
D.	Software Developments by Vendors	19
E.	Software Developments for Specific Applications	22
F.	File Organization for Effective Searching	25
G.	Entry to the File	28
H.	Summary	36

Three

Entry to the File   37

A.	The Entry Procedures	37
B.	Sample Data for Entry Analysis	38
C.	A System of Analysis Programs	38
D.	Specific Randomizing Algorithms	41
E.	Entry Analysis Results	42
F.	Summary	46

Four
Moving About within the File   47

A.	The File Design	47
B.	Sample Data for the Model	49
C.	Developing the Model	53
D.	Structured Information File	54
E.	Control Records	57
F.	Report Generation	59
G.	Summary	68

Five
Other Considerations   79

A.	Record Placement within the File	79
B.	Organizing by Frequency of Occurrence	81
C.	File Maintenance	81
D.	The Need for a Retrieval Language	84
E.	Summary	85

Six
Additional Structured Information File Applications   86

A.	The Structured Information File in Educational Administration	86
B.	The Structured Information File in Hospital Administration	91
C.	An Implication for Processing Large Tape Files	97
D.	Summary	102

Seven
Summary   123

Eight
Suggested Problems   126

Bibliography   129

Appendix
The Ten Trial Randomizers and Their Results   135

Index   159

List of Tables

Table 1. Randomizing Evaluator Summary
Table 2. Trial 2 Results
Table 3. Trial 7 Results
Table 4. Trial 9 Results
Table 5. Randomizing Evaluator Package Cost Summary
Table 6. Randomizing Evaluator Package Time Summary
Table 7. General Record Format Common Elements
Table 8. Product Data
Table 9. Salesmen
Table 10. Production and Warehouse Facilities
Table 11. Products Sold by Salesmen
Table 12. Warehouses: Quantity On-Hand
Table 13. Facilities: Quantity On-Hand
Table 14. Warehouse Requirements
Table 15. Facilities: Productive Capacity
Table 16. Transportation Costs (as Percent of Produce Cost)
Table 17. Records and Generated Home Addresses
Table 18. Product Record
Table 19. Product Disk Records
Table 20. Salesmen Record
Table 21. Salesmen Disk Records
Table 22. Facility Record
Table 23. Facility Records—Product Data
Table 24. Facility Records—Warehouse Shipping Data
Table 25. Warehouse Record
Table 26. Warehouse Disk Records
Table 27. The Control Record
Table 28. Sales Analyses
Table 29. Stock Status—Quantities On-Hand
Table 30. Transportation Costs: DH-15 Tractor
Table 31. Transportation Costs: DH-17 Cotton Picker
Table 32. Transportation Costs: DH-19 Reaper
Table 33. Transportation Costs: DH-31 Baler
Table 34. Warehouse List Without Structure

List of Tables

Table 35. Warehouse List Alpha Structured
Table 36. Warehouse List Frequency of Occurrence Structured
Table 37. Warehouses Structured by Frequency of Inquiry with Addresses
Table 38. Updated Warehouses Structured by Frequency of Inquiry with Addresses
Table 39. Trial 1 Results
Table 40. Trial 2 Results
Table 41. Trial 3 Results
Table 42. Trial 4 Results
Table 43. Trial 5 Results
Table 44. Trial 6 Results
Table 45. Trial 7 Results
Table 46. Trial 8 Results
Table 47. Trial 9 Results
Table 48. Trial 10 Results

Structured Information Files

One

Introduction

A. PURPOSE OF THIS BOOK

Information files are a major concern to all corporations. They represent the storehouse of the lifeblood of the organizational body. Without adequate data, the body dies, albeit slowly. With adequate data, the body grows and reaches for maturity and organizational continuity.

These information files reach enormous size. As they grow, the management loses the perspective of what the information was created for, how and where it is kept, and most importantly, what to do with it.

Data processing, with the particular emphasis on computers has added to the complexity. These machines, and the personnel resources that support them, are expensive and often mis-understood. Under the pressures of cost-benefit analyses, the data processing team must produce results.

The key element to producing substantive results is to integrate specific categories of data, judiciously manipulate them, and then feed the management team with meaningful information. The integration of data in a realistic, meaningful situation requires that these data file categories exist. They do exist in the business environment. They also took years and large sums of moeny to develop.

Systems analysts and programmers in the business environment have these data available to them as they develop integrating management information systems. At the same time this is usually the first exposure to computer applications that requires such integration. But, the company has both the data and large scale hardware and storage to handle the task.

Conversely, the student seldom has either the data or large scale data storage capabilities available to him. Therefore, the student is limited to learning just those applications that are either purely computational (such as engineering tasks) or to investigating those information processing techniques where the data are sequential in nature.

The basic purpose of this book is to transcend this learning and conceptual gap. Contrasts will be drawn between typical sequential processing concepts and those where random processing is essential to manipulate a *structured information file*.

A structured information file is a set of categories of data which are related to one another within the category and between categories. These relationships or linkages are constructed to permit logical manipulation in an economic and efficient fashion. The data and their categories are all stored in a random access device.

The method for organizing these data has two very distinct prongs. The first is concerned with entering the file, i.e., how to identify a particular piece of data. The second prong is the movement inside the file. Concepts in the book are presented in a specific context, in terms of actual computer programs. Included are the results of their operation on illustrative applications. The text therefore provides experimental verification of the validity of several of the propositions concerning information files.

The purpose of this book is not an overall view. It is limited to the selection and description of one method and demonstrates that it is feasible. Thus other topics with a global view must be left untreated. The typical user of this book should have had programming exposure—perhaps at this time interested in enlarging his scope of knowledge in the field of data processing by focusing on the area of information files.

Naturally, the audience is not the experienced, high level systems analyst. Indeed, they might be disturbed at some of the omissions. But it should bridge a gap that exists in EDP education between early exposure and practical applications of third generation hardware. Greater degrees of specific information develop as the reader progresses. Those interested in casual study of the subject will do well to read the introductory materials and to follow what others have done in this field. They should not be concerned with the detailed results described in later chapters.

B. THE NEED FOR INFORMATION

Executives and administrators of industry and technology in the last twenty years have faced the problem that with technological progress has come a flood of new information for professionally trained personnel to absorb.[1] Correspondingly, diversity and growth of organizational activity created a mass of administrative data for the manager. Although necessary to translate executive

---

[1] S. Stuart, "Crystal Balling: New Challenges for Chief Executives," *Infosystems,* January, 1973, p. 22.

duties into action, the vast magnitude of data has surpassed the human processing capability.

Control systems have been established to consolidate data within a firm and to meet the complex needs of management. Multiliferation and elaboration of these systems has been precipitated by human limitations in dealing with great volumes of information. Until the recent past, this problem was usually solved by organizational changes. People and work were organized in such a way that a balance could be set between the data to be processed and the human capabilities to do it.

The application of technology to information processing has been rapidly advanced, both in theory and hardware, since World War II, with the most common manifestation the electronic computer.

Early approaches to the solution of management information needs by computer were simply individual applications converted to automatic data processing. Examples of the piecemeal approach included inventory and material control, accounting and payroll, personnel, sales analysis, etc. More recently, attempts have been made to integrate such fragmented operations into a single computer-based "total information system" for monitoring the activities of the firm.

The total system philosophy has been criticized partly because the approach is inadequate and can lead to additional management problems. The total system approach is not a panacea and one should not assume that system analysis is the most important or only approach. The entire scope of management information requirements cannot be encompassed in one system.[2] The tremendous gap between planning and reality may mean that management is without an information system over a period of years and yet there is no assurance that the system will ever be satisfactory.

In an administrative environment, certain dimensions and features of information requirements cannot be subordinated to the total information system's view. One dimension is the need for varying degrees of data specificity for different functional aspects of management. A more adequate view of management information systems should revolve about a meaningful segregation of these functions. A leading authority has categorized the management functions in three levels, each with significantly different information requirements.

    1. Strategic planning which consists of (a) determining corporate policies and objectives, (b) deciding on any changes in these policies and objectives, and (c) deciding on the resources to be devoted to attaining these objectives.

    2. Management control, which consists of (a) dividing the strategic plans into logical subdivisions, (b) providing the funds to carry out the subdivisions of

---

[2] J. Dearden, "MIS is a Mirage," *Harvard Business Review,* January-February, 1972, pp. 90–99.

the plan, (c) assigning the responsibilities for carrying out each of the subdivisions of the plan to some individual, and (d) following up to see that the assignment is being carried out satisfactorily.

3. Operational control which consists of (a) determining the specific men, equipment, material, and information necessary to accomplish the subdivisions of the plan, (b) assigning these resources so that the plan can be carried out in the most efficient manner, and (c) comparing actual results with plans and taking corrective action where appropriate.[3]

Once this categorizing or separation of management functions is accepted, two steps are necessary to ascertain the potential use of computerized information systems. These are:

1. Reduce the management functions in terms of information required.
2. Review the characteristics of information systems that make them most adaptable to automation.[4]

Review and analysis of a computerized system will ascertain the degree of improvement in delivering data items and information to management over the predecessor system. Further, the review should indicate how the system enhances the ability of management to carry out assigned activities.

The inherent capabilities of the computer make it more suitable for certain applications than for others. For example, computers can process bits of data at speeds measured in millionths of a second and execute arithmetic operations with near-flawless accuracy. When combined with a storehouse consisting of vast arrays of data, the computer can perform repetitious operations and produce logical decisions based on programmed instruction and calculations. It is also possible to integrate numerous variables while processing the data.

Therefore, these characteristics suggest that some management functions can be adopted and solved by a single management information system although it will not fill the requirements of each and every category of information needs. Thus, the most useful and valuable information systems are those that recognize these distinctions.

The computer is well suited for the application and solution of many operational control problems, but it is not equally applicable for information requirements of upper management such as long range planning where the solution time is far less urgent. It is therefore not practical to develop one advanced system that attempts to meet all levels of management information requirements. The effort in developing automatic systems should be directed toward improving and refining techniques for use in operational control situations as a separate entity.

---

[3] J. Dearden, "Can Management Information Be Automated?" *Harvard Business Review*, November-December, 1962, pp. 129-30.
[4] *Ibid.*, p. 129.

C. HARDWARE DEVELOPMENTS

A rapidly emerging area of management activity revolves about the design, implementation, and use of information systems. Development has progressed along two broad fronts. The first of these is concerned with computer hardware.

Hardware is defined as "the collection of physical components which may be combined to form a computer system."[5] This will include all of the electronic, electrical, mechanical, and magnetic devices that are combined to form the physical aspects of the computer installations.

Research has yielded significant improvements in computing equipment. Faster computer speeds and expanded memory capacities, among other developments, have occurred so rapidly that it is now customary to speak of generations of hardware or machines. Advancement in this area has from the beginning surpassed the development of supporting program systems which represent the second front and are generally referred to as the software side of computer technology.

Software is defined as "the programming aids supplied by the manufacturer or developed by the user to facilitate the user's efficient operation of equipment. It includes assemblers, compilers, generators, subroutine libraries, operating systems, and industry application programs."[6] In other words, software really is the logic of the "system" from the information flow viewpoint and represents the concepts, the program, or the instructions to the machines that make them work.

Developing software often involves program applications and methods of organizing data. These data may be organized and stored as files or cards, tapes, or on mass memory devices. Each of these storage media has advantages and disadvantages which indicate specific use for specialized problems.

The first method of storing data began with the punched card. Beginning in the 1880's, more and more business applications and operations were converted to this system which led to faster and more accurate handling.

There were and are disadvantages and limitations in the 80-column Hollerith punched card for the evolving information processing tasks.

1. The size of the card limits the data that can be recorded.
2. The cards are relatively easy to lose or misplace.
3. The paper which forms the card reacts to humidity and normal manual handling, creating possible jams of the unit record machinery.
4. Large volumes of data require large volumes of cards which require large volumes of space.

---

[5] T. M. Walker and W. W. Cotterman, *An Introduction to Computer Science and Algorithmic Processes* (Boston, Mass.: Allyn and Bacon, Inc.,) 1970, p. 9.
[6] *Ibid.*, p. 774.

6 *Introduction*

5. Large card files must be sequentially processed on some of the slowest units of the modern computer.

To illustrate, the retrieval of a single unit record of data must be done sequentially as illustrated in Figures 1 and 2. However, one can enter the card file manually and extract a chosen record.

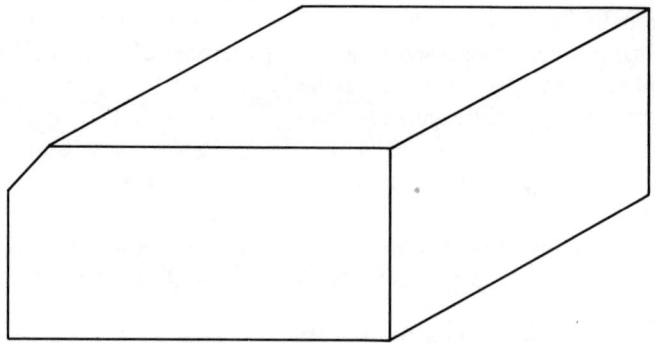

Figure 1. *Sequential card files.*

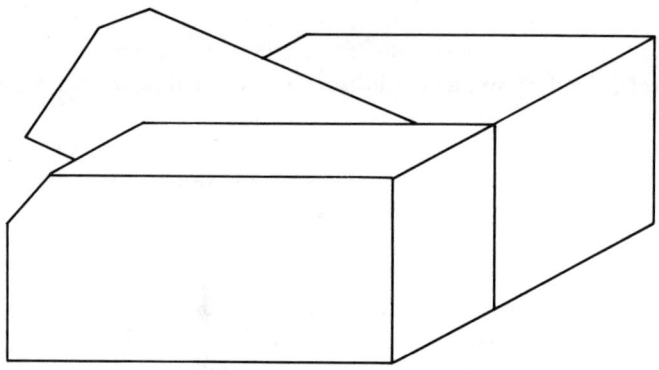

Figure 2. *Card file record retrieval.*

The development of tape files permitted the storage of large volumes of information in compact, easily stored containers. Each piece of data was stored on the tape by a magnetic "bit." Each tape is one-half inch wide and may come in lengths of 1200, 2400, or 3600 feet. The tape is contained on a reel ranging in diameter from eight to twelve inches. Data are retrieved from a tape sequentially. To select an item from the tape file, it is necessary to examine all items preceding the desired item.

Figure 3 illustrates the tape file in sequential form. Figure 4 describes how a desired record must be reached. Manual retrieval is impossible since machines are required to interpret the electronic bits of data on the magnetic tape.

Hardware Developments 7

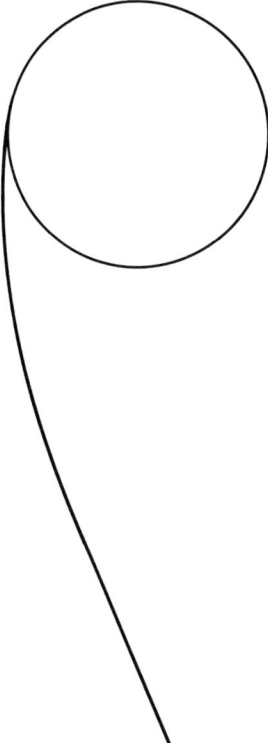

Figure 3. *Sequential tape file.*

While the processing of tape files is sequential, it is done at considerably higher speeds than manipulating cards. Tape files are actually stored in areas adjacent to the main computing unit and must be physically placed on the tape handling units. In both tape and card storage some relative delays are necessary because of the manipulation involved.

To alleviate the problems of data availability, on-line memory files are used when the need warrants.

One type of random access device is a disk pack. This resembles a stack of record platters located one above another. Data are recorded electronically on the surfaces of these platters. Each platter is divided into grooves or concentric circles onto which data are placed. Conceptually, this may be shown in Figure 5. The arms move in and out to place the read-write heads at the appropriate groove.

Each groove, then, might be divided into sections containing a fixed number of characters of information. Figure 6 illustrates this point. Thus with a stack of platters, it may be stated that one could locate any desired record if:

8   *Introduction*

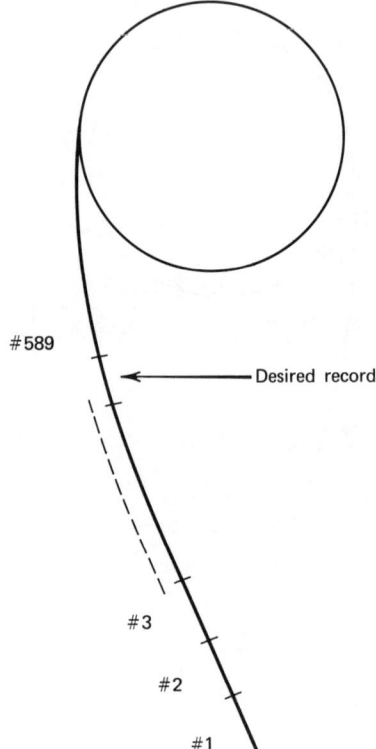

Figure 4.   *Tape file record retrieval.*

1. the platter surface were known (2 digits)
2. the concentric groove were known (2 digits)
3. and the section were known (1 digit).

The design of a practical, working file system must include or at least consider a specific, random access device. One such device, the IBM 2311 disk-storage drive allows random access memory units to be removed and changed rapidly. The flexibility of these units is comparable to a tape system but offers the advantage of direct-access processing and virtually unlimited storage. The disk storage drive is shown in Figure 7.

A disk pack resembles a stack of six platters. Each platter has recording tracks pictured as concentric circles located one above the other. There are 203 concentric cylinders each containing 10 data tracks.[7] It is shown in Figure 8.

The storage capacity of each disk pack is 7.25 million alpha numeric characters.[8] With the potential for contamination on a high density recording

---

[7] *IBM System 360 Disk Operating System Data Management Concepts* (White Plains, N.Y.: International Business Machines Corp., 1966), p. 37.

[8] *Ibid.*, p. 38.

Figure 5. *The disk concept.*

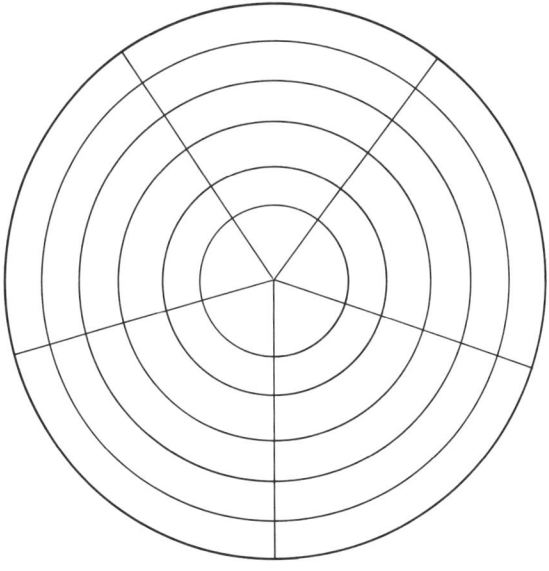

Figure 6. *The surface-groove-section concept.*

10 Introduction

track, three additional tracks are provided to ensure that the stated capacity will be available on 200 of the tracks. The user determines how the data records are organized on the memory unit based on the application of the information.

The input-output function is performed by read/write heads that are mounted and aligned on a vertical assembly. The entire assembly moves horizontally to any of the 203 cylinders. An entire cylinder is thus available for input or

Figure 7. *The IBM 2311 disk storage drive.*

Figure 8. *The IBM 1316 disk pack.*

output when the assembly of heads is electronically selected and moved into one of the ten data tracks.

A random access file is capable of storing up to one billion pieces of data. Random access storage is ". . . a type of storage in which access can be made directly to any storage location regardless of its position whether absolute or relative to the previously referenced information."[9] Data items therefore, may be processed in a logical sequence without concern for the location of the item.

Two inherent difficulties preclude widespread adoption of random access. First, it is expensive, and secondly, large scale, random access files create new problems in programming and data organization. For example, decisions must be made as to where in the file the data should be placed for a minimum of location time and yet permit additions and deletions to be made with relative ease.

---

[9]P. Fisher and G. Swindle, *Computer Programming Systems* (New York: Holt, Rinehart and Winston, 1964), p. 632.

Retrieval time for the information must not be elongated beyond acceptable bounds.

Perhaps the most difficult problem of a random file is locating stored data. Records in these files are typically identified by a number or key that is a characteristic of the record.[10] This may, for example, be a particular factory part number, hospital drug number, or a student identification number. From this characteristic number, location in the memory files can be determined precisely for retrieval. The conversion of the original number into the required machine address is often a difficult problem and if random processing of data is to succeed with random access files, a solution must be derived that is both effective and accurate.

A key distinction between sequentially processed information files and those that are processed randomly is the capability to integrate and cross-reference related items, classes, and levels of information. Thus the sequentially processed file is referred to as an unstructured file and the randomly accessed as a structured information file.

D. UNSTRUCTURED VERSUS STRUCTURED FILES

Tape-oriented files processed sequentially cannot provide cross-indexed analyses without major duplication. Related files must be searched independently or sorted into appropriate sequence to achieve desired results. An example of an unstructured data file is the effort of the librarian in processing new literature. Unstructured files are utilized by libraries faced with a flood of material. The first step is the review of the document. The contents must then be described in an abstract and transcribed to a mechanized information retrieval scheme.[11] When a need for information in a particular field arises, the user must inquire in the same terms that were used by the abstractor, and if the same key words are not employed during the search, then some pertinent literature will not be retrieved.

The depth and breadth of cross-referencing that is necessary for inter-relating all the literature in a store such as a library is a problem of enormous magnitude. This enormity, with the associated high costs, results in library files remaining basically unstructured. This is not to suggest that libraries are not indexed, but that a sequentially arranged information bank does not yet mechanically cross-index the classes of information and makes information retrieval dependent on the compatibility of storage and inquiry terms.

A second example of the difficulty with the unstructured file occurs in education. In this area four classes of information are germane:

---

[10] G. Davis, *Computer Data Processing* (New York: McGraw-Hill, 1973), p. 356.
[11] B. Cheydleur, "Information Retrieval, 1966," *Datamation*, October, 1961, p. 24.

1. data about the pupils
2. data about the courses
3. data about the teachers
4. data about the schools.

These four files may be maintained separately or incorporated within one file. Because the latter can become excessively bulky the former method is usually selected for tape files. This is shown in Figure 9.

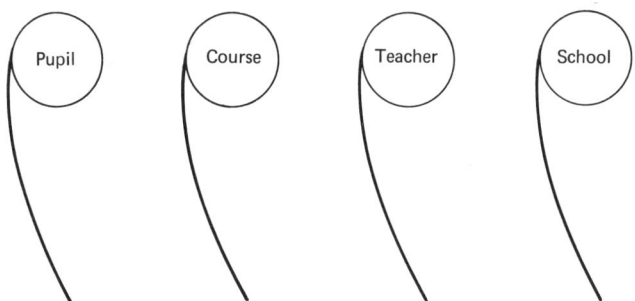

Figure 9.   *Tape files isolated by class.*

The difficulty with a cross-file analysis in an unstructured organization is diagrammed in Figure 10.

One must search sequentially through the pupil file until the desired student's record is reached. Data in that record would define what course the pupil is taking which, of course, means that that file must be searched. Data in the course record will define the teacher and college for that course. Thus both of these files must be searched respectively until the appropriate records are reached. When the examination is complete for this one course for this one student, the course file, teacher file, and possibly the school file must be rewound to examine the student's second course. While not particularly difficult to do physically, this process is time-consuming and expensive in terms of elapsed time and complex instructions.

Conversely, structured files offer significantly more advantages. Recall that a structured file contains the logical ties between related data items and allows these data to be processed randomly. Related information can be considered as classes or levels of data. Each level is related to other members of that level and to other levels by common terms previously stored and the nature of the application.

The major purpose of a structured information file is to provide logical links between and among various levels of information. Once this file is established, it is possible to manipulate and examine data in any combination and in any sequence.

If an item belongs in a class of information, it will be referenced with that class. Unlike information retrieval using unstructured files, data would not be subject to abstracting errors of interpretation because it is not necessary. Hence,

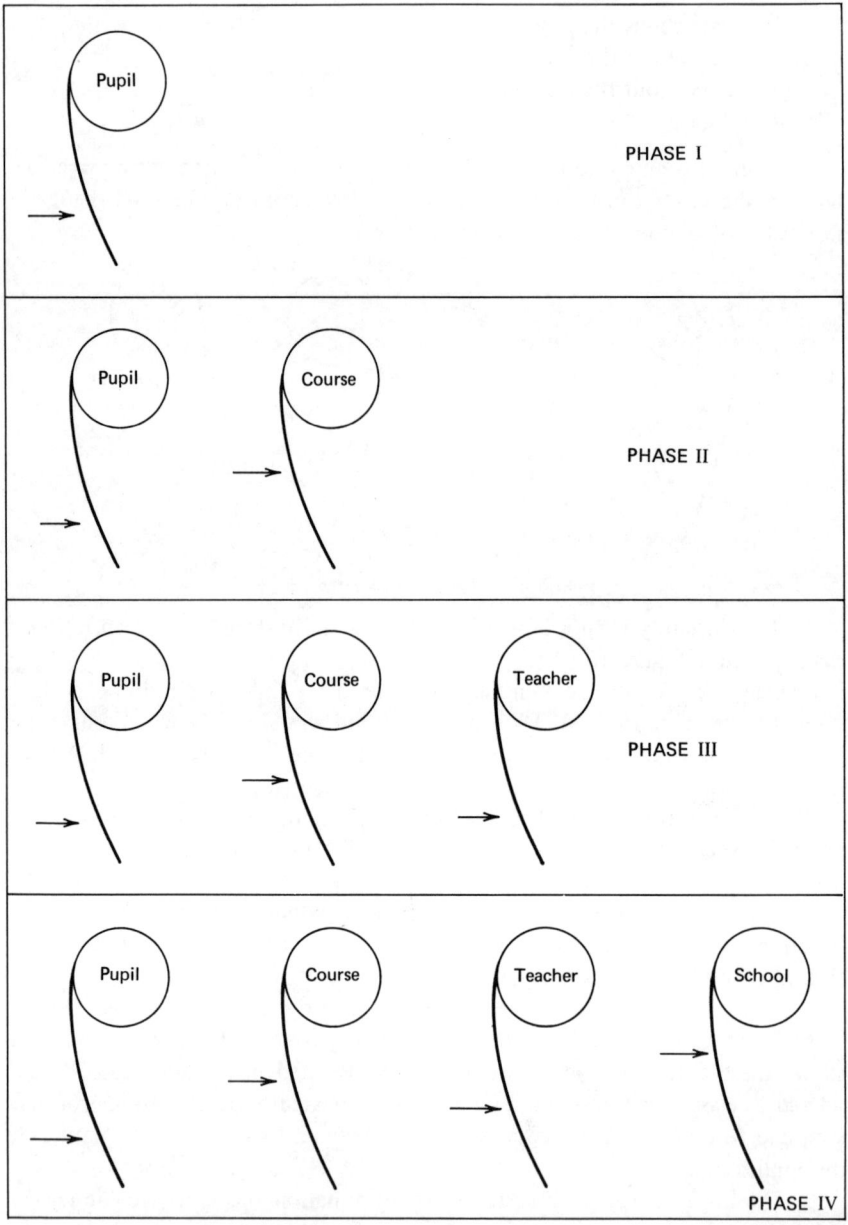

Figure 10. *Searching tape files.*

no pertinent or related items would be omitted when a level or class of data is searched.

An example of a simple structured information file in business is the bill-of-materials in a production environment. Each final product is composed of a variety of subassemblies and each subassembly is produced from components. Each component is described by lower level parts. This breakdown, level by level, continues until the lowest part number is reached. A lowest level part number is one with no further lower level components and this may be either a raw material or a purchased item.

A second example of a structured file in a business situation relates the basic classes of information necessary for product distribution. These classes of data are usually: salesmen, production facility capacities, warehouse facility capacities, and products. These strata would be linked to each other by order of descending involvement and interface.

In an academic setting, an educational structured information file might include such basic strata of data as students, courses, teachers, and schools. Each student would be related to the courses he is enrolled in, to the professors who teach these courses, and to the colleges in which the courses are offered. Still another example of a structured information file might be the medical profession where the data might relate: doctors, patients, drugs, and facilities.

The two file concepts, unstructured and structured, actually serve different purposes. If management requirements for an information system involved thoroughly related data, then a structured file must be adopted. Unstructured, tape-oriented files do not possess an integrating capability. A structured information file would contain the pertinent data and relationships necessary for operational control uses.

Thus, at the operating level of management the structured file concept is applicable, whereas the unstructured files would be of minimal value.

E. SUMMARY

If the task to be automated, i.e., computerized, requires a large amount of sequential processing, then the problem is relatively simple. Paryoll and insurance record keeping are two such examples. An unstructured or sequential file would suffice.

If, on the other hand, only a small percentage of the records are to be processed, then the file design problem becomes much more acute. A method must be established to permit random entry and effective movement internally, with effective linking and communication with stored data having common relationships. Thus, a structured file utilizing random access disc storage would provide this capability.

Two

Background

The prime purpose of this book is to demonstrate the design and use of a structured information file. One method of examining design criteria is to compare and study what has been done. A set of these designs can then be gathered together to form the basic model.

A. THE INTERDEPENDENCE OF STORAGE AND RETRIEVAL

The ideal management information system provides rapid and accurate data gathering, storage, and retrieval activities.[1] Unfortunately, an economic restriction is placed on many retrieval systems because the vast networks of data lack regimentation and organization. This basic flaw is exemplified by the inability to interrelate one logical record segment with another and because of the task of identifying and indexing the factual content.[2]

While it is basic to organize, interrelate, and store data, it is equally necessary to retrieve them. Storage and retrieval must be examined as an inseparably interdependent entity. A definition of a data retrieval and storage system is ". . . an organized method for storing data in a manner which permits or facilitates their recall or retrieval from storage."[3] This definition specifically identifies that the two components must be treated as a single system and not as a separate storage and a separate retrieval system.

---

[1] P. Margaritis, "A Real-Time Management Information Retrieval System," *Data Processing Magazine,* July, 1965, p. 23.
[2] *Ibid.*
[3] M. Taubes and H. Wooster, *Information Storage and Retrieval,* (New York: Columbia University Press, 1958), p. 19.

Because the storage of information on mass random access discs is more costly than on magnetic tape, consideration must be given to the distinction between general activity and segregated activity.[4] The major characteristic of the general activity is the use of batch updating of the information file since time is not a factor. A segregated activity requires specific data on a timely basis, and processing data through a structured file concept attains the maximum benefit of an operating system.

B. RANDOM AND SEQUENTIAL FILES

To establish and maintain control of operational activities, most information processing systems utilize random rather than sequential processing. This choice requires that the master files be organized in a specific manner.

The choice of a suitable type of processing operation dictates how the master file is to be organized and the sequence in which the detail transactions are processed. Two modes of processing, random and sequential, are available:

> *Random processing* is the processing of detail transactions against a master file in whatever order the detail items occur. In *sequential processing* the input transactions are grouped together, sorted into master file control-number sequence, and the resulting batch is then processed against the master file.[5]

Sequential processing is most commonly adopted when the master file information is on cards or tape. This is not to suggest that processing can not also be accomplished with random access storage units, but, by storing the master file on disk, alternative methods may be chosen. It is the nature of the application that should dictate the choice.

When time is not a factor, the detail data are batched, sorted into control number order, and processed sequentially against the master file. However when this time delay is unacceptable, random processing offers the solution. This on-line availability of information, however, is paid for by the increased cost per unit of data stored.

On-line data are usually stored in a mass-memory medium, or storage unit, in what is identified as a logical file. A related sequence of records is a logical file.[6] Each record is assigned a control number that specifically represents one and only one record in the file. Each record is stored at a specific location

---

[4]Margaritis, *op. cit.*, p. 23
[5]*Disk Storage Concepts* (White Plains, N.Y.: International Business Machines Corp., 1963), p. 7.
[6]Davis, *op. cit.*, p. 316.

identified by the memory address. As an example, in an IBM 1405 disk storage unit the address is a five digit number.[7]

A logical file can be arranged within the storage unit in two basic ways, sequential and random file organization.[8]

> In a sequential file records are sorted and stored in the disk storage unit in control number sequence so that records with successively higher control numbers have successively higher addresses.[9]

The control number and the home address are not likely to be the same number, and while they are not necessarily consecutive, the control numbers and home addresses must be sequentially ascending.[10] Locating a record in the sequential file is accomplished by finding the control number in an index and then seeking and retrieving the record at the home address specified by the index.

> Random file organization is substantially different.
>
> In a random file each record is stored at an address computed by a randomizing routine. That procedure calculates the address from the item's control number. The order of the record within the storage unit with respect to their control numbers is determined by a formula and therefore the file is generally not sequential.[11]

A record in a random file is located by computing its address from the control number using the identical algorithm utilized to store the record.

C. CHARACTERIZING STORED INFORMATION

The procedure by which stored information is catalogued is known as indexing. This effectively consists of maintaining the file sequentially or randomly (ed.) and keeping a directory or an index to the file.[12] The index is searched by the program for the desired key and corresponding disk address.[13] The indexing process covers a wide range of functions. It may relate factual data by unique identification such as names of persons or things, or assign classification or subject readings for descriptive articles and books.

Two distinct problem areas occur when information systems are automated.

---

[7]*Reference Manual 1401 Data Processing System* (White Plains, N.Y.: International Business Machines Corp., 1961), p. 59.

[8]Davis, *op. cit.,* pp. 354-356.

[9]*Disk Storage Concept* (White Plains, N.Y.: International Business Machines Corp., 1963), p. 7.

[10]*Ibid.*

[11]*Ibid.*

[12]W. Price, *Introduction to Data Processing* (San Francisco: Rinehart Press, 1972), p. 226.

[13]*Ibid.,* p. 227.

The first concerns operations related to the content of the documents and the second involves the physical processing of the documents.[14] The latter is a problem best solved by the equipment designers. The content of the document can be best identified by the primary characteristics that satisfactorily describe the meaning that was intended to be conveyed.

A content analysis involving a frequency of work occurrence is a basic approach.[15] The resultant vocabulary and the frequency of occurrence provide descriptors for the major ideas of the document. A comparison of the vocabularies of two stored documents might establish their similarity and result in a similar-meaning document being retrieved. The number of words can be reduced by disregarding classes of words. Results using only twenty to thirty highest ranking words have produced adequate results.[16]

A typical application of this procedure is the IBM Key-Word-In-Context or KWIC system. However, the general acceptance of keyword indexing is significantly hindered by three items, i.e., the lack of depth in the indexing, the rate of growth of the file to be examined, and the location of the index with respect to the data file.[17] Since the index is most frequently external and separate from the information file, "successful" inquiry into the index only retrieves a citation to a potentially useful document rather than an immediately useful datum.[18]

D. SOFTWARE DEVELOPMENTS BY VENDORS

Manufacturers are aware of the need for software developments possessing the capability of random access file processing. The International Business Machines Corporation has developed a system of programs that will perform the functions of data file establishment, maintenance, and retrieval for its current hardware. The stated purpose of GIS (Generalized Information System) is to provide ". . . exceptional facilities for creating, maintaining, and processing data files as well as retrieving data.[19] The goal of this development effort is to permit the user to design a data base for specific tasks and to achieve implementation rapidly. IBM responded to the need caused by staff growth in the complex busi-

---

[14] H. Luhn, "Automated Intelligence Systems—Some Basic Problems and Prerequisites for their Solution," in E. Tomeski et al. (ed.), *The Clarification, Unification, and Integration of Information, Storage, and Retrieval* (New York: Management Dynamics Corp., 1961), p. 9.
[15] *Ibid.*, p. 10.
[16] *Ibid.*
[17] A. Opler, "Information Retrieval by Digital Computer—Reality or Myth," in E. Tomeski, et al., *op. cit.*, p. 70.
[18] J. Costello, "Indexing in Depth: Practical Parameter," in P. Howerton *Information Handling: First Principles* (Washington, D.C.: Spartan Books, 1963), p. 55.
[19] *Generalized Information System* (White Plains, N.Y.: International Business Machines Corp., 1971), p. 1.

ness environment. To provide the managerial statistics, reports, and forecasts, these staff groups were forced to gather, maintain, and retrieve large volumes of data. The concept of the Generalized Information System is an attempt to develop a general solution that can be applied to each of the specific problems. A further development, GIS/2 adds greater flexibility and integrates with other IBM information management schemes.[20]

Government departments were faced with many of the same problems of information handling. To support the variety of nationwide and worldwide government functions, vast data banks are required. Some data are required on a real-time basis such as national defense, while others such as social security perhaps are less urgent and may be processed sequentially. The generic solution for developing systems to meet many various needs has not been agreed upon.

Two extreme approaches have been utilized in the implementation of data processing.[21] In one, operations were analyzed and independent activities were converted to data processing on a piecemeal basis. Executed under a monitor control system, new capabilities or functions required new programs or re-programming added to the system.

The second or total systems approach was the other extreme where the entire system was designed, programmed, and implemented in a single entity. As long as the operating environment remained relatively stable, this has some chance of justifying the large capital outlay and interruption of procedures during implementation.

In a proper climate, it is conceivable that either or both of the approaches would be useful and sound. However, the climate is seldom stable enough to offset the significant disadvantages of each. With a dependence on well-defined and stable data, problem specification changes and data changes can be accommodated only with significant elapsed time delays and man time in programming or re-programming. An emerging third approach to application programming is known as the "evolutionary approach."[22] It is based on a structured file of information with generalized logical relationships that allow the preparation of most information processing tasks.[23] Sufficient flexibility allows new applications and modifications to be implemented with a minimum of re-programming.

To utilize the evolutionary approach the systems designer must identify the required data and their manipulations and construct a data base for the tasks to be accomplished. New applications utilize the existing data base and avoid the major task of creating new master files.

---

[20] *Generalized Information System/2* (White Plains, N.Y.: International Business Machines Corp., 1971), p. 1.
[21] J. Salzer, "Evolutionary Design of Complex Systems," in D. Eckman *Systems: Research and Design* (New York: John Wiley and Sons, Inc., 1961) pp. 200–201.
[22] *Ibid.*, p. 202.
[23] *Generalized Information System* (White Plains, N.Y.: International Business Machines Corp., 1971), p. 1.
[24] Margaritis, *op. cit.*, p. 23.

In 1965, a General Electric plant reported a successful real-time retrieval procedure using a GE 225 computer and a mass random access memory system.[24] The success of the procedure was attirubted to the initial design when time cataloging standards were introduced. Each file was referenced by logical file name and a unique field code within the file. The data were arranged according to specific control classes which in turn were indexed for each data element in the logical file. Nominated data were easily retrieved by referencing the three-character alphanumeric code and examining the items within the class until the appropriate record was reached.

General Electric has recently been engaged in the development of a concept called Integrated Data Store to rival the Generalized Information System concept of IBM.

> The Integrated Data Store is a computer language designed to facilitate the organization, storage, maintenance, and retrieval of information using a mass memory storage medium.[25]

Integrated Data Store is designed for use with COBOL and is not in itself a data storage and retrieval system. It is designed to offer the user the opportunity to develop logical record relationships not specifically available in COBOL.[26]

Earlier General Electric had been involved in the development of decision tables that had their roots in the Report and File Maintenance Generators derived at Hanford, Washington.[27] The culmination of that effort was a system 9PAC, a report generator for the IBM 709. It was best suited to serial file processing.

In 1964, the National Cash Register Company introduced a problem-oriented file design. Subsequently, the activities of file creation, file maintenance, and data manipulation and retrieval have been integrated within the language architecture of their current hardware.[28] This was project Business EDP Systems Technique or BEST. BEST was not to be implemented as an on-line system, but was specifically designed to develop problem-oriented solutions for rapid and efficient implementation.

A key requirement in developing the system was a decision on file organization.[29] The solution was to treat separate logical information files as independent files which might interact with each other but only in one direction. For example, data from the personnel file would be available to the organization file through a logical link. There would not be a logical link in other directions, however.

---

[25] C. Bachman, "Integrated Data Store," in C. Baum and L. Gorsuch (ed.) *Proceedings of the Second Symposium on Computer-Centered Data Base Systems* (Santa Monica, Calif.: Systems Development Corp., 1965), p. 3.231.
[26] *Ibid.*
[27] *Ibid.*, p. 3.232.
[28] *NEAT/3* (Dayton, Ohio: National Cash Register Co., 1968), pp. 5–13.
[29] *Ibid.*

E. SOFTWARE DEVELOPMENTS FOR SPECIFIC APPLICATIONS

Numerous administrative disciplines are examining the use and application of software for retrieval and storage with a minimum of exchange of developments between and among these groups. A review of the literature reveals a significant duplication of effort. Several applications in various disciplines are discussed in the following.

The basic product discriptor in manufacturing is the bill-of-materials.[30] The parts list, as it is alternately known, provides both a manufacturing description and a cost analysis. Since it contains the full list of parts and reference drawings, the bill-of-materials is the spare parts catalogue for the customer. The apparent simplicity of a parts list is not borne out upon careful analysis. Each list requires a serial listing of all parts and subassemblies as well as the quantities of each required to produce each unit. Since many parts might be used at various levels of the manufacturing assembly, the final bill-of-materials contains a number of interlocking and cross-referenced parts lists. This needs to be represented in the structured information file approach. From this, each place a part is used and the effect of producing a given number of the end product can be ascertained. Further breakdowns such as exploded parts drawings can be developed.

When stored sequentially on magnetic tape, a great amount of record duplication is required. Random access units permit the structure to be constructed without the duplication and substantially aids production activities.[31]

The International Business Machines Corporation has developed a program that establishes the bill-of-materials file and maintains it. The concept was originally designed for implementation on an IBM 305 RAMAC system used in the late 1950's. IBM expanded the system to contain other facets of manufacturing management information. This more comprehensive form, was titled Management Operating System (MOS).[32]

Educators' uses of information are often similar to those of businessmen. Research in educational information systems has been conducted at many institutions. Two examples are the Iowa Educational Information Center at the University of Iowa and Project Talent of the University of Pittsburgh. Educators use information for longitudinal studies and logistical control of the student population. This presents a distinct problem for the system designer. This unique need is reflected in the Project Talent philosophy towards the data bank concept.

Although the term data bank usually refers to a process of gathering and storing data, the designer must be aware that certain data subsets will be of greater value than others. Perhaps a better definition of the data bank would limit the term to those data collected ". . . with some overall basic design and

---
[30] C. Bachman, "Software for Random Access Processing," *Datamation,* April, 1965, p. 36.
[31] *Ibid.,* p. 37.
[32] J. Hartmann, "Management Control in Real-Time Is The Objective," *Systems and Procedures Journal,* September 1965, p. 27.

for which research uses were originally considered."[33] It is not implied that only research purposes need be served by these data. To the contrary, it reflects the adherence to sound research principles during the data collection process.

There are at least seven characteristics that a useful research data bank possesses.

1. The data must represent a well-known target population. The importance of randomness in research data samples can not be over-emphasized. The need for nearly complete population representation in operational control situations also cannot be over-emphasized.

2. A wide range of specific observations is desirable. Broad band width is necessary if the bank is to be applicable to a variety of research or operational control questions.

3. Costs of data collection must be considered. By pooling resources through the cooperative efforts implied in data banking, the required volume of data can be collected and deposited.

4. The data must be easily accessible. Modern methods of data processing and information retrieval can make large volumes of data accessible in a reasonable amount of time.

5. Comparable data are essential if generalizations are to be extensive. Many large stores of data are limited to usefulness because the types of data collected or time of collection vary.

6. Ease in record linkage is essential for the expansion and improvement of longitudinal studies.

7. Links must be provided for data collected at one time with data about those same subjects studied or collected at another time.[34]

Hospitals now make extensive use of on-line data management systems. A time-shared computer in Cambridge, Massachusetts, services 48 remote location teletypes that are on-line to a centrally located computer.[35] These offer program and retrieval opportunities for the hospital administration without the redundant investment in on-site computers. The initial use of the computer was to study the feasibility of hospital administration and medical applications on a real-time (concurrent) basis.

> The system consisted of three basic information handling operations. First, the description of the format and structure of the data; second, the assimilation of the data into the computer (according to that description); and third, the retrieval of the stored data.[36]

---

[33] J. Flanagan, *The Project Talent Data Bank* (Pittsburgh: University of Pittsburgh, 1956), p. 1.

[34] *Ibid.*

[35] P. A. Castleman, "On-Line Data Management System for the Massachusetts General Hospital," C. Baum and L. Gorsuch (ed.) *Proceedings of the Second Symposium on Computer Centered Data Base Systems* (Santa Monica, Calif.: Systems Development Corp., 1965), p. 3.143.

24   Background

The first operation is of major concern. The file itself is stored on a 50 million character Univac Fastrand drum with each record variable in length consisting of chained 150 character blocks. The structure of the file is more concerned with the content and arrangement within a record rather than the logical ties between a record, thus the logical structure is single level. Retrieval is performed by linear searching of the file with comparison to a selector.

With the data divided into logical files and the retrieval system able to examine one logical file at a time, a merger of two basic files is necessary to simultaneously search the related data items in each. This system restricts data searches to a two-level structure. To retrieve data from other logical levels of data or from other logical files the file must be restructured for the particular retrieval.

A 1963 study by analysts of the System Development Corporation (SDC) Santa Monica, California, reported an investigation of the application of electronic data processing to the field of medical data.[37] At the outset, simulation and modeling seemed to offer promise but it soon became apparent that the administrative needs of the hospital were more pressing. Patient data was given priority because of the vast array of information required for appropriate patient care.

The analysis of hospital data processing utilized a twofold approach.

> First, a system design team composed of SDC and Veteran personnel was formed to conduct analyses of certain facets of the hospital in terms of its functional system requirements, information demands, and concomitant data flow rates. Secondly, a system development team composed of SDC and VA personnel was formed to conduct the on-going equipment and simulation studies required to support the design effort.[38]

These two groups arrived at a basic objective that the hospital data system was to achieve,

> It must relieve the clinician and other professional personnel from routine tasks associated with the collecting, recording, storing, summarizing, retrieving, transmitting, and displaying of data that are used directly or indirectly in proving medical and administrative care to the patient.[39]

The simulation study led to the determination of six major areas of hospital activities.

1. Patient admissions and dispositions.
2. Inter-ward transfers and discharges.

---

[36] *Ibid.*, p. 3.144.

[37] H. Wilson, "A Hospital Patient Data System," *Data Processing for Management*, May, 1963, p. 22.

[38] *Ibid.*, p. 23.

[39] *Ibid.*

3. Laboratory tests.
4. Vital signs.
5. Medications.
6. Administrative statistics.[40]

These analyses depict the degree of specificity that is required by the hospital patient information system. The data must provide a complete and up-to-the-minute statement of conditions of both the patients and the hospital's facilities. A data processing system designed to automate the six major hospital activities would be of the operational control nature as previously defined.

The legal profession with a vast spectrum of cases to examine has adopted unstructured retrieval techniques. Today's lawyer is confronted with constant change and expansion of statutory, decisional, and regulatory material. Many of these legal systems are an aid in research problems but because of searching delay time are not sufficient for problems where minimum response is an essential factor.[41]

F. FILE ORGANIZATION FOR EFFECTIVE SEARCHING

The nature of the searches for the operational control decision maker is well-defined and has short time constraints.[42] Current efforts to develop such systems have been undertaken to satisfy the minimum response time requirements. This file system should exhibit the following characteristics.

1. Extensive data on a narrow range of subjects.
2. The data are evaluated prior to addition to the file.
3. The data have limited and well-defined relationships.
4. Inputs to the file may be fragmentary.[43]

A search of an integrated file thus becomes little more than a well-defined clerical routine that is easily adaptable to processing by computer, but the clerical procedure must be effective and efficient. Four basic parameters of effective information searching for decision makers have been set forth by the federal government. They are completeness, relevance, timeliness, and form of system response.[44]

---

[40] *Ibid.*
[41] For a discussion on legal storage and retrieval systems see "Computer - Assisted Legal Research," *Oregon Law Review,* Summer 1972, pp. 665-696.
[42] J. Garland, "Optimizing Information Searches," in P. Howerton, *Information Handling: First Principles* (Washington, D.C.: Spartan Books, 1963), p. 96.
[43] *Ibid.,* p. 97.
[44] U.S. Senate, Committee on Government Operations, *Coordination of Information on Federal Research and Development Projects in the Field of Electronics* (Washington, D.C.: Government Printing Office, 1961), p. 146.

Completeness refers to methods of assuring that all the information in the system on the subject has actually been retrieved. Relevance is a method of increasing the yield of information directly proportioned to the searcher's original requirement from the total retrieved. Timeliness is reducing the turn-around time from request to response. Form of system response is the method of delivery of the information in the most usable manner.[45]

The parameters of effective searching suggest an approach to the problem of file organization. To develop a satisfactory and valid control scheme, proper consideration must be given to user requirements and the identification of a rigorous method of analyzing the subjects. A suggested method for a logical construction plan would contain the following steps.

    1. An understanding of the commonly accepted categories for dividing the characteristic of a given field of knowledge.

    2. Isolate every distinctive category and recognize every relation between and among categories.

    3. Organize the categories into suitable divisions and assign an order in which the divisions are to be used.

    4. Fit the schedule of divisions with a notation that will permit the fully flexible combination of terms that is needed.[46]

The combination of algorithms and hardware enables a search of large blocks of data quickly and efficiently and they must be able to follow a path of logical relationships very rapidly. Discussion of these relationships appears in the technical literature under the heading "associative memories."[47]

Associative memory stores possess three basic properties.

    1. Linkage of related items in storage.

    2. Parallel search capability over all or part of the memory at a given time.

    3. Distributed rather than centralized control for parallel processing.[48]

The linkage property is usually described in software terms as list, structure, or threaded lists. This framework suggests the existence of some logical relationship between items. The linkages are so constructed that it must be possible to get from any one item to any other related item below or above it on the list structure. (Figure 11 displays the concept of logical chain linkage.)

This capability of relating any item in a data subset with any other item in the subset is termed end-linking. A chain is created when the last item in the

---

[45] J. Garland, *op. cit.*, pp. 97–98.
[46] P. Atherton, "File Organization," in P. Howerton (ed.), *Information Handling: First Principles* (Washington, D.C.: Spartan Books, 1961), p. 47.
[47] For example, see D. Reich, "Associative Memories and Information Retrieval," M. Kochen, *Some Problems in Information Science* (N.Y.: Scarecrow Press, 1965), p. 217.
[48] *Ibid.*

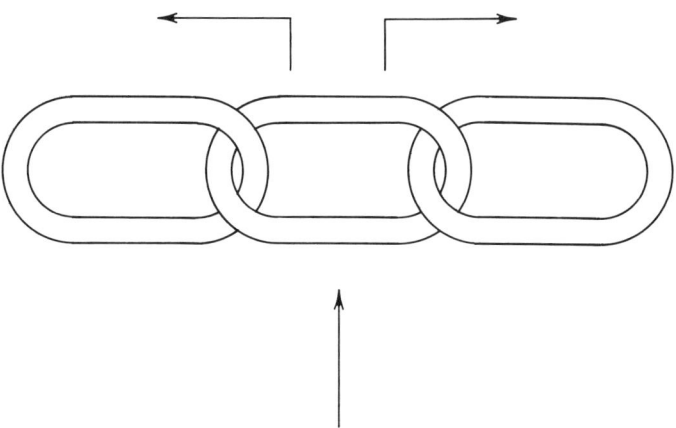

Figure 11. *Logical chain linkage.*

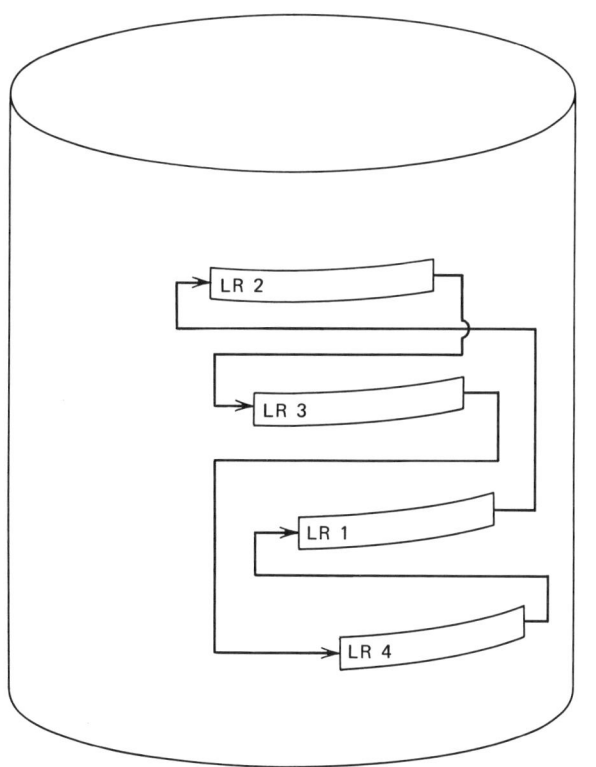

Figure 12. *Circular association of logical records.*

list is linked to the first item. The examination of the whole set is then a relatively simple clerical procedure accomplished by machine regardless of the point of entry into the chain.

Figure 12 is a graphic example of logical record linkage with four logical records located randomly within the random access device. For simplicity, they have been labeled LR1 for logical record 1, LR2 for logical record 2, etc. The chain linkage is created by relating LR1 to LR2, LR2 to LR3, and LR3 to LR4. The chain is end-linked by logically connecting LR4 to LR1 thus completing the circular association.

The chain is the primary data organization linkage by which many structured file schemes link a group of related records.[49] By storing the address of a succeeding record within the record of a preceding member, the tie is created. Thus, a circular association of related records may be threaded together.

G. ENTRY TO THE FILE

Associative memory or chain link concepts lend themselves to effective and efficient file analysis. However, the means of entry to a segment of the chain such that analysis may begin must be determined. Three particular techniques are usually suggested. One of these is termed "randomizing," the second is "indexing,"[50] and the third is termed index sequential.

Randomizing is the method whereby an identification number of a desired record is obtained in some manner to produce an address within the memory file. Although this may not be the correct address, it served at one time as the record address, either at storage time or in a subsequent search. The record at that memory address is then examined and the identification number of that record is compared to the criterion record in the new search. This comparison is necessary because it is possible that duplication will occur when reducing a number in size from nine digits as an identification number to five digits as a home address in the memory file. That is, more than one identification number can be randomized to the same home address. To alleviate this condition, it is necessary to provide an overflow or synonym address. The overflow or synonym address specifies a new record to examine. Thus, a chain of addresses is created all of which are accessed from the randomizing procedure which directs attention to the initial home address.

Figure 13 is an example of this procedure. The number 390-38-4227 is the identification number of the desired record. By a randomizing algorithm of some

---

[49] See for example, R. Kaimann, "Project TUHL: An Integrated Educational Data Bank," in *Automated Education Handbook* (Detroit: Automated Education Center, 1965), pp. VI A 23-31.

[50] The writer gratefully acknowledges the permission granted by North American Publishing, Inc., to reproduce this material that originally appeared under his name as "Entry to the File: Randomize or Index," *Data Processing Magazine,* December, 1966, pp. 18-21.

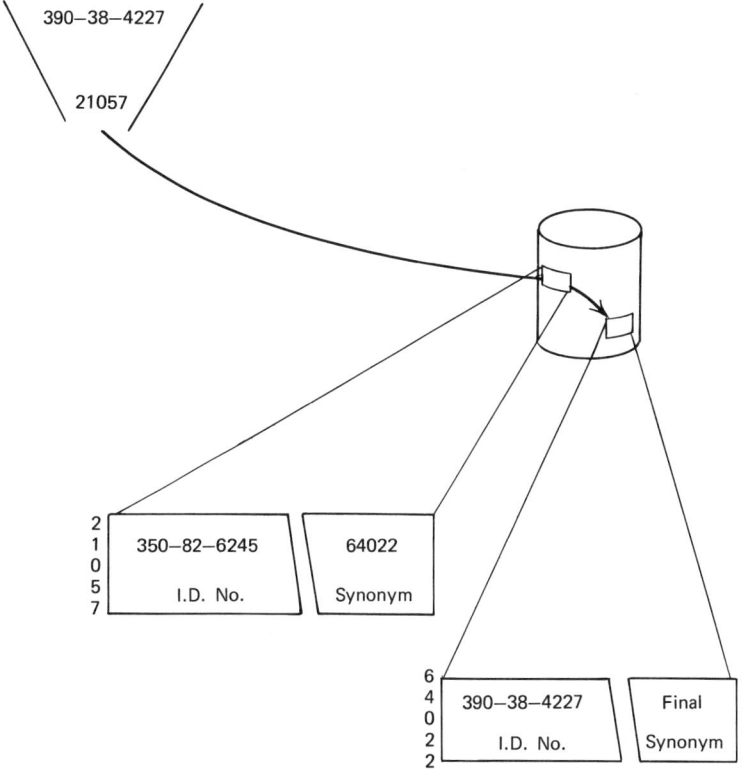

Figure 13.   *Randomizing.*

kind, this nine digit number is reduced to a five digit number, i.e., 21057. This number is termed the generated home address. The search procedure begins there. The record located at 21057 in the file is accessed. A segment of that record is the identification number for that record. It may be that the proper record has not yet been reached and in our example, this is the case, as the identification number of the first record accessed is not the same as the criterion identification number. Since the proper record has not yet been reached, a synonym or overflow address is contained in the record. This number, 64022, indicates that access should be made to the record located at the home address where another record is stored that had originally randomized to the 21057 generated home address. The record at 64022 is then accessed and its identification number is examined and compared with the criterion number. It is shown that now a match has been found so that the appropriate record has been reached. The synonym of this record would be another home address or if no other identification numbers had randomized to 21057, an end-of-chain sentinel could be stored there.

The indexing technique incorporates a separately maintained table of the

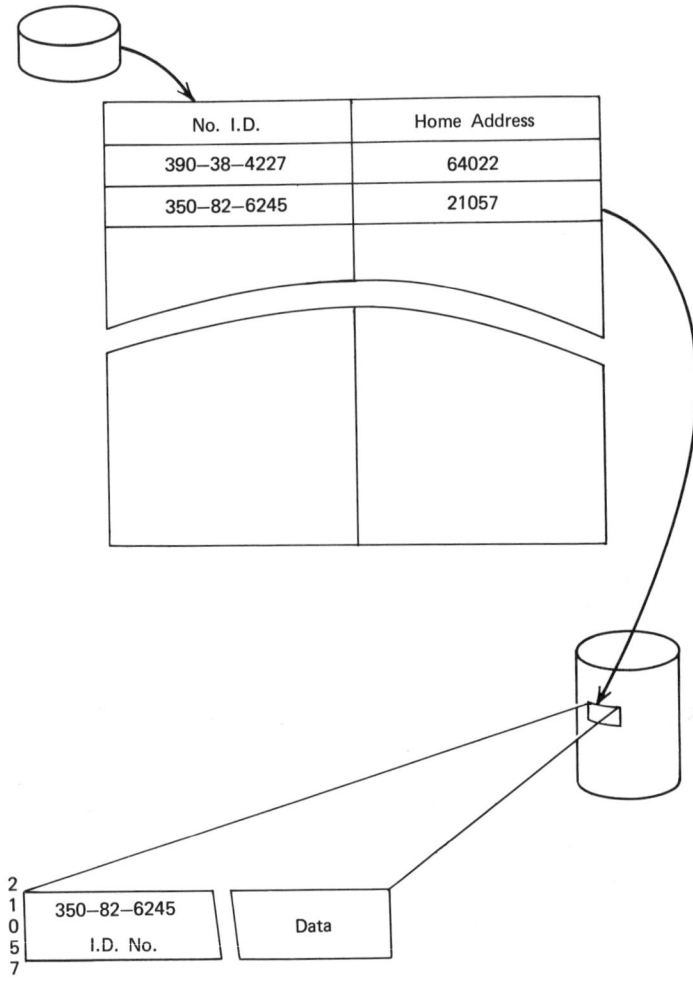

Figure 14. *Indexing.*

identification numbers.[51] Each identification number identifies the home address in the memory file. When an inquiry is necessary or a criterion record is desired, the index is searched and when a match is found the home address is automatically identified and access can be made directly. Figure 14 is an example of this procedure. In this example the criterion record desired is identified by the number 350-82-6245. The file is entered at the beginning of the table and the identification number is compared with the criterion record. This is not a correct match in the first case so the second identification is searched. At this point, the correct identification number has been found. The appropriate home

---

[51] Costello, *op. cit.*, p. 56.

address is shown as 21057. This address would then be accessed and the identification number in that record would be compared with the criterion identification number to assure that the proper record has been accessed.

The third method of accessing stored data is index sequential. This method employs a sequentially organized file with rapid retrieval capability. The storage device is the random access concept with the access arms on each level moving synchronously. For example, assume the access arms move to track 5 on surface 3. Since the arms are all attached to one moving mechanism, all the read-write heads move simultaneously. Further, the disk surfaces are continually rotating, creating a kind of cylinder of information. With vertical and horizontal orientation any data can be input to the system merely by specifying the appropriate surface. This is shown in Figure 15.

Data are stored sequentially by moving the arms to one track and then sequentially storing on that track. When the track is filled to capacity, storage continues on the next surface but still the same track number. Thus, the data are

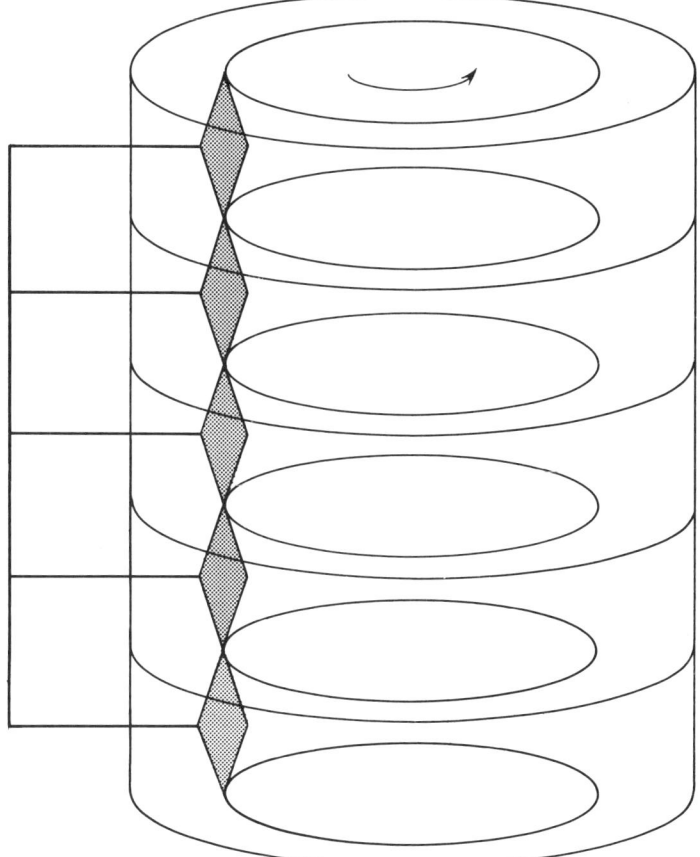

Figure 15. *The cylinder concept.*

created as a "cylinder" formed by the circularity of the disc and the verticality of each track. This is shown in Figure 16. Once all the tracks are filled, the access arms move to the next track and a second "cylinder" has data placed on it, creating a sequential file.

To retrieve data at random from the index sequential file requires a set of referencing indexes. For example, a cylinder index is stored on the first cylinder of the file. This index contains the highest reference number stored on each cylinder. Once an index search reveals the correct cylinder the access arms move to that cylinder.

A surface index is found at the head of each cylinder. The surface index contains the highest reference number stored on each surface. Once the correct surface is selected, that specific read-write head is activated, causing all ten sectors to be examined. When the correct sector is found, it is input for processing.

As an example, assume a sequential file of 10,000 items is stored in sequential fashion. Further assume a storage device with 10 surfaces, 200 usable tracks, and 10 sectors per track. Now suppose record 493 is required for processing. The access arms are directed to the first cylinder. The cylinder index is examined. Figure 17 displays the cylinder index.

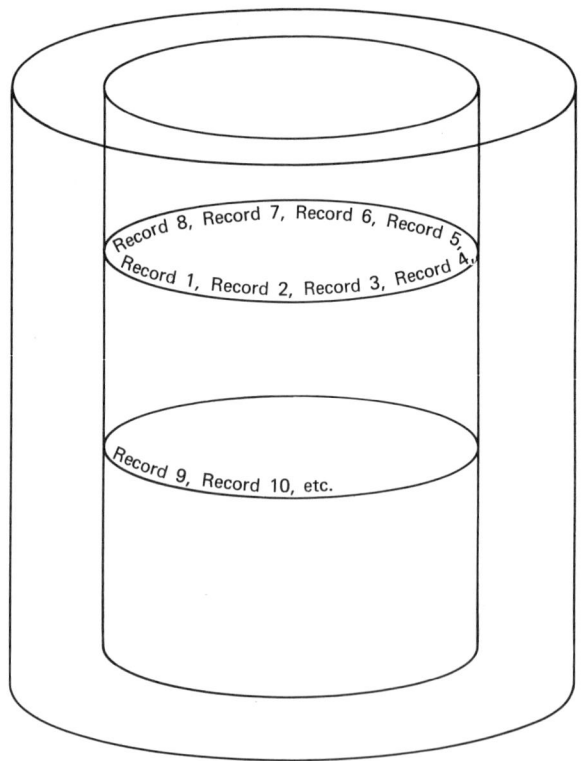

Figure 16.   *Storing data on the cylinder.*

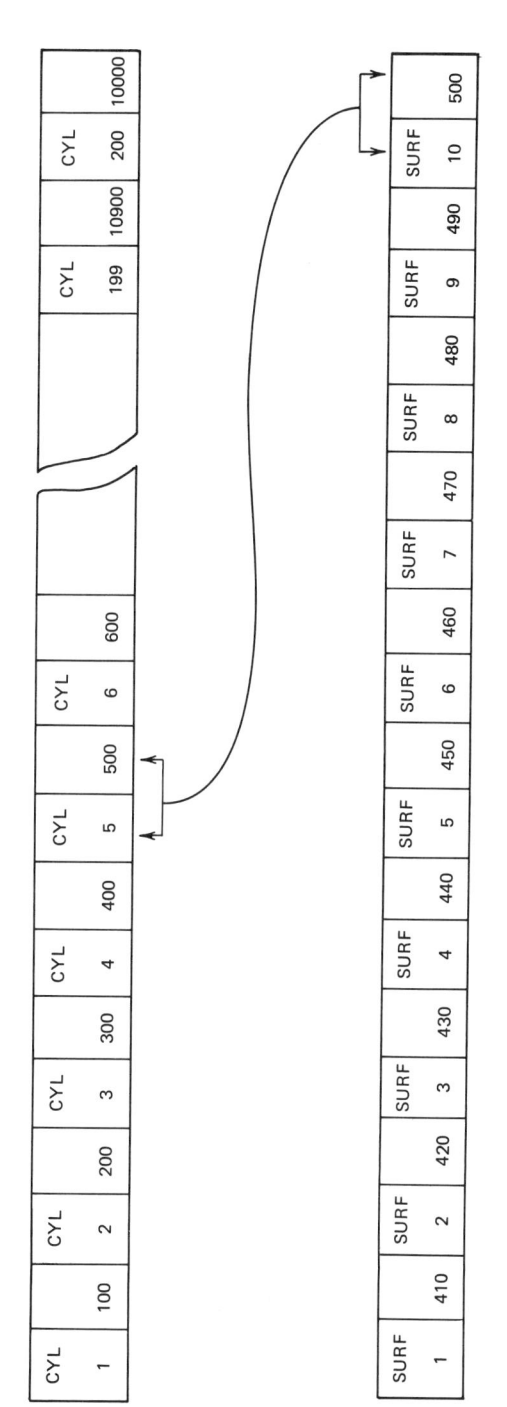

Figure 17 (top). *The cylinder index.*   **Figure 18 (bottom).** *The surface index.*

34   Background

By examining the index for the highest record in each cylinder, it is seen that record 493 is on cylinder 5. The access arms are directed to move into position to read the surface index for that cylinder. That index is shown in Figure 18. The surface index indicated that the appropriate record is contained on surface 10. Thus the read head for surface 10 is instructed to read the track given by cylinder 5 and surface 10. The organization of the records on that track is shown in Figure 19. Each record is examined until the desired record (number 493) is found. It is now available for processing.

The index sequential methodology is popular for two very good reasons. First, it permits random access to files that are basically of a sequential nature. Secondly, most of the vendor software support the index sequential approach. Yet the method may be weaker in the future. More and more applications are

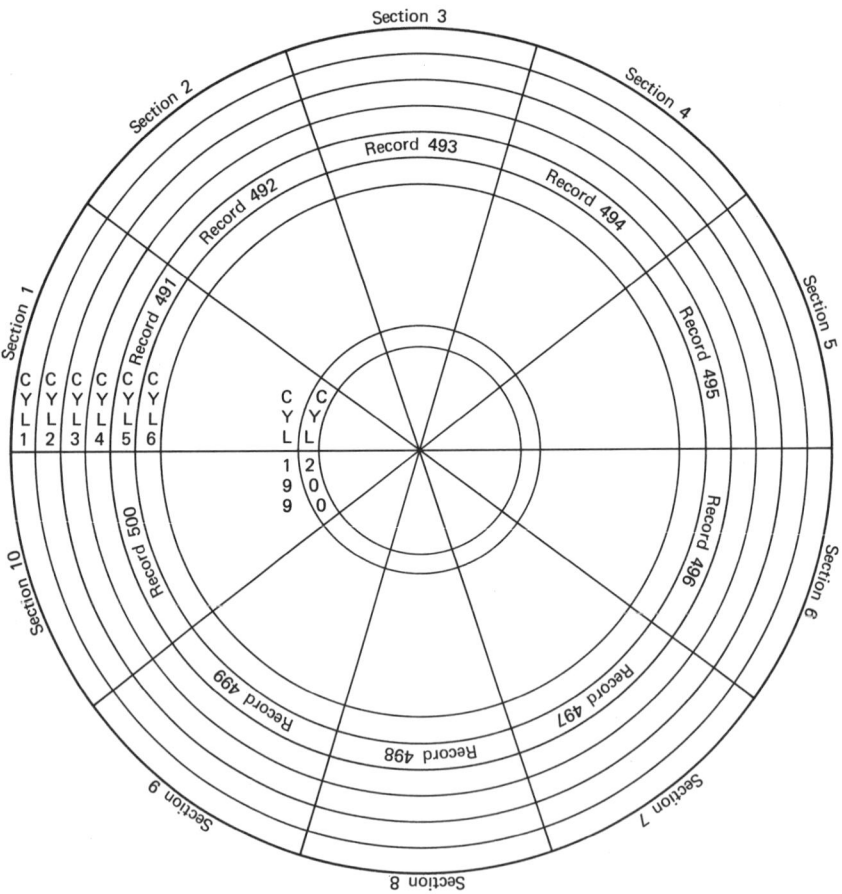

Figure 19.   *The records in the section of cylinder 5, surface 10.*

being implemented where the characteristic number is not meaningful to the processing. In a bill-of-materials for example, there is little relation between the numeric value of a part number to any other number in the bill-of-materials. Thus, in applications where sequential processing is not the principal manipulation and where the characteristic numbers are not meaningful, the index sequential approach is weaker than traditional random processing.

When it is desired to locate information in memory associated with a given identifier, access to the information should be very rapid. The less complex techniques of table-look-up or binary searches are too slow.[52] The derivation of adequate transformation functions for converting a key into an address may be time-consuming and difficult. However, if it is discovered, the retrieval of nominated records may be performed very quickly and with a minimum of wasted memory capacity.

To be ideal for use in storage devices, the techniques for generating the home address should produce each home address within the proper range once and only once. There would be no duplications. In practice, this is never the case and some duplications always exist, causing some unused space.[53] For example, assume two unique records with different control numbers both convert to the same home address. The first record occupies the storage location. The second record must be stored in a different, unused location. This displaced record is termed an "overflow record."

As has been noted, chaining is a technique for handling overflow by referencing the address of another location where the second record has been placed. If there had been three unique records that had converted to the same home address, the chaining technique would be extended. The first record occupies the home address. An overflow address is stored in a field of the first record that directs attention to the location of the second record. The location of the third record is stored as the overflow address of the second record and so forth. Thus, the chain contains records logically connected with the initial home address serving as the beginning.

Certain basic techniques have been suggested for identifying the home address by manipulating the characteristic number. Typical of randomizing methods that may be tried are:[54]

1. Division. If the number of memory locations is N, the characteristic number may be divided by N with the value of the remainder being used as the randomizing address.

2. Division by a prime number. A good distribution is often discovered

---

[52] J. Beatty and S. Muroga, "File Memory Addressing," in M. Kochen, *Some Problems in Information Science* (New York: Scarecrow Press, Inc., 1965), p. 206.
[53] *Ibid.,* p. 208.
[54] J. Martin, *Programming Real-Time Computer Systems* (Englewood Cliffs, N.J.: Prentice-Hall, Inc., 1965, pp. 111-112.

if the division is by a prime number. The prime number used should be slightly less than the number of memory addresses available.

3. Truncating. A quick form of the division technique is to divide by 100, 1000, 10,000, etc. This accomplished a truncation of the reference number and the required number of low order digits are retrieved as the home address.

4. Extracting. If some of the digits suggest that they will have a better distribution than others, these may be isolated and used by themselves. Thus, if some digits of the characteristic appear more important than others, only those particular digits need be used.

5. Squaring. The middle digits of the square of the characteristic number may be utilized as the home address.

H. SUMMARY

This chapter has examined several areas pertinent to the topic of the structured information file. The relationship between storage and retrieval is inseparable. Data processing might be carried out randomly or sequentially with two general classes of file organizations. For operational control situations, where rapid retrieval of data is necessary, random processing of randomly organized files appears superior.

Both users and vendors are engaged in developmental efforts to harness the data within the administrative unit. The results of these singular efforts are viewed on a whole to select respective strengths for the developments of the structured information file philosophy. Although records within the file are logically linked together, it remains necessary to access the data by some type of entry procedure. Three techniques, indexing, randomizing, and index sequential, are discussed.

The next two chapters of the book are quite specific. The two elements of file design, i.e., (1) entry to the file, and (2) moving about internally are described in terms of both the conceptual and the actual. They are presented in a high degree of specificity to show the depth of involvement required.

Three

Entry to the File

We have defined computer-stored information manipulation as a two-fold problem. The first part of this is the recovery of a previously stored data item or entry into the file. The second part concerns the logical associations between records or how do you move around logically once you are inside the file.

This chapter describes the entry to the file from the outside. The following chapter will consider movement within the file.

A. THE ENTRY PROCEDURES

The randomizing technique is accepted as one method for entry to the file. In the true random processing concept described earlier, it was suggested that randomizing was superior to other entry schemes. To prove that randomizing is superior, one need only derive one randomizing algorithm that is better than the optimum capability of the other methods. The criterion for judging the value of each technique is the average number of accesses required to reach any nominated record. Since the index is usually maintained separately from the main data, at least two accesses are required with the indexing procedure. Under optimum conditions, the first access would seek and retrieve the index and the second access would seek and retrieve the nominated record. In index sequential, one seek and read is required to fetch the cylinder index, and another seek is usually required to reach the correct cylinder. The surface selection and section selection will not require additional seeks, only extra reads. These will not be counted for the minimum criteria. Thus, the minimum for index sequential is also two seeks and reads. If one randomizing algorithm can be derived that produces an average number of accesses that is less than two for a particular sample population, then it can be described as superior to indexing.

This claim would not be valid if an algorithm is not found that yields an average number of accesses less than two. This conclusion could not be drawn until an infinitely large number of algorithms had been evaluated and the only conclusion that would have been reached is that an adequate algorithm has not yet been discovered. In this case, the user may well decide to utilize the indexing procedure and abandon the search for a potentially more efficient randomizing algorithm.

B. SAMPLE DATA FOR ENTRY ANALYSIS

Entry procedures can be best evaluated using typical item identifiers encountered in actual situations. Assume that a population of about 50,000 entries is being considered. Further assume that a random access device such as an IBM 1301 with 100,000 sectors is available. Hence, five-digit home addresses will be required. This allows an initial packing density of .5 with room for potential expansion.

For the purposes of this example, a sample population will be used. During 1965, the Iowa Educational Information Center administered the Card Pac pupil personnel inventory of public school elementary and secondary students. Approximately 600,000 records were identified. Of those, 48,950 had taken either the Iowa Test of Basic Skills or the Iowa Test of Education Development and were in Title I programs. This proportion of 1/12 of the pupil population was selected for entry procedure analysis.

Each pupil is identified by a unique nine digit number, the first four high order digits represent the school district and the last five digits identify the pupil within the district. These identification numbers are characteristic numbers to be evaluated by the randomizing methodologies.

Only the identifier numbers need to be converted to machine usable form at the outset. Since the entry analysis precedes the file creation, the remaining or "heavy" data conversion should be delayed.

C. A SYSTEM OF ANALYSIS PROGRAMS

There are three segments that comprise the analysis of randomizing procedures. These are discussed in the following in terms of a tape-oriented IBM 7044. The set of programs is designed to function as a single system. A systems flow chart of the procedure is presented in Figure 20.

The first program contains the specific randomizer routine. This routine converts the raw data from a nine digit number to a five digit number. These data are then written on a magnetic tape that becomes the input for the second program.

A System of Analysis Programs

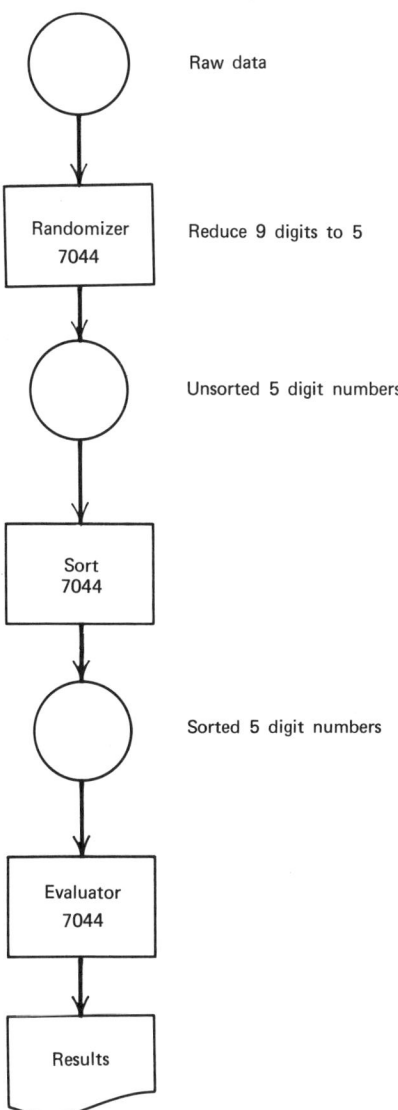

Figure 20. *Evaluation package systems flowchart.*

The second program is a sort routine from the 7044 library. The unsorted five digit numbers are sorted into ascending sequence and the sorted output becomes input for the third program.

The third program is the evaluator. An evaluation of the trial randomizer consists of counting the frequency of occurrence of each of the number of synonyms and determining the average number of accesses required to locate any nominated item.

40   Entry to the File

Before discussing the actual randomizing process, consider the procedural aspects of using the three program system. The first program, the randomizer, should be written in a modular fashion so that different trial randomizers may easily be inserted. This allows the evaluation package to be run by merely inserting the randomizer in position and placing a run identification card at the back of the entire package. This is illustrated in Figure 21.

The evaluation program develops a frequency of synonyms table. Each generated home address is read from the sorted tape and accounted for in the tabulation. If a large number of identification numbers generate the same home address, it is possible to exceed the limits of the table. To accommodate this contingency, all such occurrences will be placed in a general category at the bottom of the table. Zero to 200 synonyms will be allowed with the "over 200" category following. If that were to happen, it is probable that that randomizer would not be selected, so this eventuality is not bothersome.

The actual evaluation process begins when the data have been completely entered in the frequency table. By summarizing the frequency of occurrence entries, the number of unique home addresses is determined.

The total number of accesses (TA) in our example is determined by the formula:

$$TA = \sum_{I=1}^{200} \frac{I(I+1)}{2} \times N_I + 201 \left[48,950 - \sum_{I=1}^{200} (N_I * I) \right]$$

where: N_I = the number of synonyms in this subset. This method of reaching the total number of accesses is necessary for two reasons. First, the number of contributing members to any synonym subset must be determined. Then, in each subset, it is necessary to determine the number of accesses to reach each member in that set.

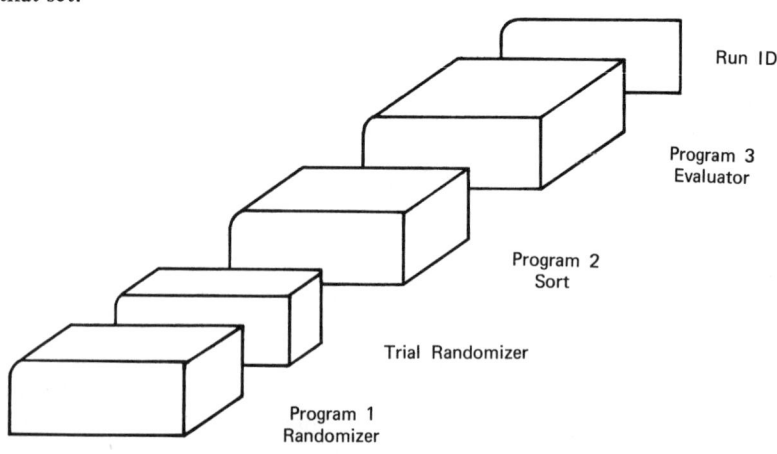

Figure 21. *Evaluation package program deck structure.*

For example, if there are 1,000 occurrences of zero synonyms, then each of the 1,000 contributors would be located with the first access. If there are 150 occurrences of one synonym then there are actually 300 contributors. Of these 300, 150 would be reached on the first access but 150 would require two accesses to be reached. Thus, the total number of accesses required to reach each of the 1,300 contributing items would be (1,000) (1) + (150) (1) + (150) (2) = 1,450. The average number of accesses is determined by dividing the total number of accesses by the number of contributing items.

D. SPECIFIC RANDOMIZING ALGORITHMS

In the following, ten specific algorithms are developed and evaluated utilizing the five general techniques that have been suggested for developing the home addresses as a base. The specific techniques posited were selected on the basis of their simplicity rather than their mathematical complexity for several reasons. First and foremost, users are usually not mathematicians nor do they have the staff capability to facilitate the use of complex algorithmic techniques. Secondly, the technique should be of such a level of understandability that the systems analyst, the systems designer, and the programmer will easily grasp the concept and be able to communicate it to management if necessary.

Trial Number 1
This trial takes the remainder after division by 100,000. For example:
    I.D. Number   123456789
    Home Address   56789

Trial Number 2
This trial selects the middle five digits from the square of the characteristic number. For example:
    I.D. Number   123456789
    (I.D. No.)^2 15241578750190521
    Home Address   78750

Trial Number 3
This trial selects the five high order digits of the remainder after division by 10^6. For example:
    I.D. Number   123456789
    Home Address   45678

Trial Number 4
This trial selects the five high order digits of the remainder after division by 10^7. For example:
    I.D. Number   123456789
    Home Address   34567

Trial Number 5
This trial selects the five high order digits of the remainder after division by 10^8. For example:
    I.D. Number   123456789
    Home Address   23456

Trial Number 6
This trial selects the five high order digits of the characteristic number. For example:
    I.D. Number   123456789
    Home Address   12345

Trial Number 7
This trial selects the five digits remainder after division by the largest prime number under 100,000. For example:
    I.D. Number   123456789

$$\frac{123456789}{99991} = 1234 \, \frac{67895}{99991}$$

    Home Address   67895

Trial Number 8
This trial selects five of the six low order digits by extraction, eliminating the thousands position. For example:
    I.D. Number   123456789
    Home Address   45789

Trial Number 9
This trial selects five of the digits extracting the two low order digits of sub-field one and the three low order digits of sub-field two. For example:
    I.D. Number   123456789
    Home Address   34789

Trial Number 10
This trial selects the five middle digits of the square of the home address as derived in trial 8. For example:
    I.D. Number   123456789
    Extraction   45789
    Squared   2096632521
    Home Address   66325

    Each of the ten trials is written as a separate computer routine and inserted into the three program evaluation package. The 48,950 unique characteristic numbers are then processed by the system.

E. ENTRY ANALYSIS RESULTS

The student should note that of all the previous examples only trial number 2 would present any significant programming difficulty. Here the char-

TABLE 1. Randomizing Evaluator Summary (Sample Size = 48,950)

Trial	Generated Home Address	Total Number of Accesses	Average Number of Accesses
1	9,996	751,844	15.359
2	26,628	96,924	1.980
3	5,349	809,209	16.531
4	1,818	1,279,445	26.138
5	562	205,021,912	4,188.394
6	415	458,045,104	9,357.408
7	34,783	67,540	1.380
8	13,914	168,404	3.440
9	35,471	67,420	1.377
10	12,872	193,746	3.958

TABLE 2. Trial 2 Results

Synonyms	Frequency	Percent	Cumulative Percent
0	16649.	34.0123	34.0123
1	4490.	18.3453	52.3575
2	2219.	13.5996	65.9571
3	1405.	11.4811	77.4382
4	985.	9.0398	86.4780
5	520.	6.3739	92.8519
6	277.	3.9612	96.8131
7	114.	1.8631	98.6762
8	50.	0.9193	99.5955
9	14.	0.2860	99.8815
10	2.	0.0449	99.9265
11	3.	0.0735	100.0000
Total number of input records		48950	
Total number of home addresses generated		26628	
Total number of accesses		96924	
Average number of accesses		1.980	

acteristic nine digit number was squared and the middle five digits of the product were to be selected as the generated home address. However, a nine digit number squared yielded a possible 18 digits as a product. A result of this size exceeded the number of significant digits allowed in a 7044 word. To alleviate this con-

TABLE 3. Trial 7 Results

Synonyms	Frequency	Percent	Cumulative Percent
0	24075.	49.1828	49.1828
1	8014.	32.7436	81.9265
2	2095.	12.8396	94.7661
3	464.	3.7916	98.5577
4	107.	1.0827	99.6404
5	27.	0.3309	99.9714
6	2.	0.0286	100.0000

Total number of input records	48950
Total number of home addresses generated	34783
Total number of accesses	67540
Average number of accesses	1.380

TABLE 4. Trial 9 Results

Synonyms	Frequency	Percent	Cumulative Percent
0	25562.	52.2206	52.2206
1	7361.	30.0756	82.2962
2	1822.	11.1665	93.4627
3	512.	4.1839	97.6466
4	151.	1.5424	99.1890
5	46.	0.5638	99.7528
6	15.	0.2145	99.9673
7	2.	0.0327	100.0000

Total number of input records	48950
Total number of home addresses generated	35471
Total number of accesses	67420
Average number of accesses	1.377

dition, double precision arithmetic was used so that each value was placed in two computer memory words allowing a sufficient number of significant digits to be retained to permit the extraction of the middle five digits.

Three of the trials produced an average number of accesses less than 2.0 for this population. A set of summary tables are shown in the Appendix. You will note Table 1 summarizes these results including the number of generated home addresses, the total number of accesses, and the average number of accesses for each trial methodology and Tables 2, 3, 4 display the details from which more successful results were summarized.

It was previously stated that at least one algorithm must be found that produced an average number of accesses of less than 2.0 to accept the randomizing technique as a superior entry procedure for this data set. Trials two, seven, and nine accommodated this need. Trial two had selected the middle five digits of the square of the characteristic number and produced an average number of accesses of 1.980. Trial seven had selected the five digit remainder after division by the largest prime number under 100,000 and yielded 1.380 as the average.

Trial nine had selected the two low order digits of sub-field one (the school district) and the three low order digits of sub-field two (the pupil number within the school district). The resulting average number of accesses for trial nine was 1.377 which was the best result. For the 48,950 pupil sample, a file could be constructed in which each data record could be retrieved with 1.377 accesses, a

TABLE 5. Randomizing Evaluator Package Cost Summary

Trial	Randomizing	Sort	Evaluator	Total
1	$ 3.93	$ 6.61	$ 2.46	$ 13.00
2	21.94	8.50	2.64	33.08
3	4.70	7.80	3.50	16.00
4	4.16	8.91	5.65	18.72
5	4.89	11.45	3.46	14.20
6	3.81	7.42	2.97	19.80
7	101.35	7.35	3.86	122.56
8	5.31	13.78	5.43	24.52
9	6.46	9.33	4.61	20.40
10	5.37	11.13	3.58	20.08
Totals	$161.92	$ 92.28	$ 38.16	$292.36

TABLE 6. Randomizing Evaluator Package Time Summary

Trial	Randomizing	Sort	Evaluator	Total
1	2'38"	4'25"	1'39"	8'42"
2	14'38"	5'40"	1'46"	22'04"
3	3'08"	5'12"	2'20"	10'40"
4	2'47"	5'56"	3'46"	12'29"
5	2'33"	4'57"	1'59"	9'29"
6	3'16"	7'38"	2'19"	13'13"
7	67'34"	4'45"	2'35"	75'03"
8	3'33"	9'11"	3'37"	16'21"
9	4'19"	6'13"	3'05"	13'37"
10	3'35"	7'25"	2'23"	13'23"
Totals	108'01"	61'31"	25'31"	195'01"

definite improvement over the optimum of 2 accesses offered by the indexing technique. Thus, on the basis of the sample population utilized and for random processing purposes a randomizing entry procedure would be appropriate.

However, had no algorithm been discovered that produced a 2.0 accesses average or less the user would either develop additional trial randomizers or abandon this approach and utilize the indexing technique that is conceptually easier to prepare the decision as to which alternative to select would be dependent to a degree on the time and effort spent in the development, programming, and evaluation.

These factors can be studied by examining the time and cost analysis sheets produced by the 7044 system following each run. Tables 5 and 6 illustrate the time and cost associated with the three operations, the randomizer, the sort, and the evaluator. Based on $90 per hour a total cost of $292.36 was computed for 195 minutes and 1 second of 7044 computer time. Research, designing new algorithms, and the programming are not included in this cost analysis. This control analysis will make it evident that if simple randomizing techniques will not produce satisfactory results quickly, then substantially greater efforts in terms of time and money will be required. Further, the abstract and theoretical talents required for the more complex numerical analysis will likely exceed the ability of the average systems analyst. Although costs for processing will vary as different machines are utilized, software costs are consistently high. Thus, it is quite likely that unless an adequate randomizer algorithm is discovered early, the user will switch to the indexing methods.

F. SUMMARY

This chapter has examined three methods of gaining access to a random access file. Two methods provided a conservative estimate of 2.0 minimum seeks and reads for reaching any nominated record. A variety of randomizing algorithms were suggested and evaluated. Four algorithms produced an average number of seeks and reads of less than 2.0, which supports the theory of randomizing as a superior entry procedure to indexing or index sequential.

Four

Moving About Within the File

This chapter discusses a second aspect of file design: the internal linkages for moving about within the file. The last chapter explained entry to the file.

A. THE FILE DESIGN

A structured file that utilizes random file organization will contain a variety of records. The format of each of these related records will vary substantially, but there will be a degree of agreement on the position of some common elements. These commonalities within the records are necessary for the basic considerations of identification, association, linkage, and chaining. Five elements are common to each record category.

The first of the common elements is a check character. This single character uniquely identifies the record category. The check character is a screen because it is possible for entries in two different categories to possess the same identification or key number. For example, the nine digit social security number of a salesman coincidently might match the nine digit code assigned to a product for its identification. The check character provides a unique guarantee against such an occurrence.

The second of the common elements is record identification. This numeric field houses the full record key or identification number. It can be, for example, the product number or salesman's social security number.

The third common element is a synonym or chaining address, and contains the logical linkage to another memory location. It is utilized when the randomizing procedure provides a home address that does not contain the identification number of the nominated record. It is a link in a chain that logically relates all of those records whose identification numbers randomize to the same address.

The fourth common element is any tie that links all of the records in this category. The links in this chain might be, for example, an alphabetic or other sequential arrangement. It is significant in that a full relationship is maintained so that sequential processing can occur.

The fifth common element is a data overflow field. In this file design, each record will be a fixed size. When space is not available for all the pertinent data concerning a given record, it is necessary to store them elsewhere. The data overflow field contains a memory location for this excess data.

In addition to these five common elements, each record will contain some fields that are similar in appearance and identical in purpose, including a linkage to a record in another category and linkages that provide circular association for a subgroup within the fixed length will be dictated by the application.

With the variety of possible formats in addition to the common elements, it is desirable to select a programming language that permits redefinition of records. This is necessary because, aside from the common elements, the other data fields will be of different dimensions. Until the record is accessed and the identification examined, the user cannot be aware of the other fields.

One might choose FORTRAN and accomplish this via a REREAD using the proper format, but it would be inefficient. Micro level languages, such as AUTOCODER and BAL accomplish this easily. Yet there remains the desire to utilize the advantages of procedural level languages.

One flexibility of the COBOL language is the ability to redefine the format of a given record after it has been read. The "REDEFINES" clause permits the automatic transformation of the format and allows the addressing to be conducted by data-names that are appropriate to that particular record.

As an illustration consider a model of four disk cylinders with each record 116 characters in length. This specification is important. First, there is not an advantage to using a greater number of cylinders since the model itself will require substantially less than four full cylinders of random access capacity. Second, the time required to process large numbers of unnecessary blank records might become significant.

The selection of record length is determined by the amount of data required. A systems study would establish this requirement. However, for the purpose of illustration, the record will be displayed on the printer on one line and must be less than 132 characters in length. Although other character record lengths might be selected, 116 was arbitrarily chosen. This record length allows ten records per track. With ten surfaces and four full cylinders 400 records could be contained in the model. When involved in a specific application, a thorough investigation would be required to determine the record length. Since we are considering only the skeleton and concept of the structured information file, arbitrary record length should not be a point of concern.

Five elements have been identified as common to each record type. The

check character will occupy the first position of the record format. The identification number (assumed to be nine digits for this study) will occupy record positions 2 through 10. Positions 11-107 will contain data and linkages that are pertinent to the particular record type. The data overflow linkage occupies positions 108-110. The linkage that ties all entries in the category occupies positions 111-113. The synonym linkage occupies positions 114-116. (These common elements are illustrated in Table 7.) The linkages will require only three digits since the maximum number of logical records is 400.

TABLE 7. General Record Format, Common Elements

Field	Positions
Check Character	1
Identification Number	2- 10
Specific Record Information	11-107
Data Overflow	108-110
Category Link	111-113
Synonym	114-116

Continuing the illustration of the feasibility of the structured information file, a hypothetical, but typical business problem is formulated. This example will relate the various files associated with the product-distribution scheme in business. Four categories of information are:

1. Product-information.
2. Salesman-information.
3. Warehouse-information.
4. Production Facility-information.

Each of the categories provides particular information and provides linkage to the other categories. The design of the remainder of the particular record formats will be such that logical movement can be made between the records. Following accepted principles of data processing, data are recorded in only one location rather than in duplicate. For example, the warehouse record will identify the product housed there by the home address of the product. Further information about the product would be found only in the product record.

B. SAMPLE DATA FOR THE MODEL

The hypothetical data set will include four products, eight salesmen, four warehouses, and three producing facilities. Most of the numerical values are randomly selected. Table 8 illustrates the products and their associated identification number, description, and sales value. Table 9 displays the names of the salesmen and their identification numbers. Table 10 indicates the production and warehouse facilities with their identification numbers and locations. (These facilities represent actual warehouses and factories of a farm implement producer, the Allis-Chalmers Manufacturing Company.)

Table 11 identifies the current quantities of each product sold by each salesman. An N/A entry in any cell indicates that the salesman does not sell that

TABLE 8. Product Data

Identification Number	Description	Sales Value
231575485	D H 15 Tractor	$ 6,319.87
901837259	D H 17 Cotton Picker	7,234.76
376249708	D H 19 Reaper	9,188.99
869523036	D H 21 Baler	11,995.04

TABLE 9. Salesmen

Identification Number	Name
189975530	Ahling, Martin
870942512	Beach, Robert D.
584154882	Casey, Bernard
105131174	Esslinger, William
269381443	Haupert, Raymond B.
393087232	Nortmann, George B.
797331182	Wyjack, Harvey
264706850	Zeithamel, William L.

TABLE 10. Production and Warehouse Facilities

Production Facilities		Warehouse Facilities	
Identification Number	Location	Identification Number	Location
647558103	Gadsden, Alabama	201769977	Denver, Colorado
388584025	Oxnard, California	615655436	Dallas, Texas
122259228	Springfield, Illinois	950459344	Buffalo, New York
		594728038	Atlanta, Georgia

TABLE 11. Products Sold by Salesmen

	Salesmen							
Product	1	2	3	4	5	6	7	8
1	74	N/A*	55	N/A	55	4	31	5
2	74	N/A	8	90	N/A	18	37	44
3	10	N/A	22	11	54	38	N/A	34
4	38	97	67	49	51	94	5	N/A

*N/A indicates that the salesman is not selling that product.

particular product. Tables 12 and 13 indicate the current on-hand quantities at the warehouses and production facilities respectively. Table 14 describes the forecasted monthly requirements of each product at each warehouse and Table 15 shows the productive capacity of each product by each manufacturing facility.

Transportation costs from each point of manufacture to each warehouse are shown in Table 16 as a percent of product costs. These values are proportional to the distances between the point of origin and the destination.

TABLE 12. Warehouses: Quantity On-Hand

Warehouse	Product			
	1	2	3	4
Buffalo	99	65	21	93
Atlanta	98	12	106	203
Dallas	31	77	87	110
Denver	82	296	216	14

TABLE 13. Facilities: Quantity On-Hand

Facility	Product			
	1	2	3	4
Gadsden	024	119	482	272
Springfield	325	667	112	178
Oxnard	627	625	755	874

TABLE 14. Warehouse Requirements

Warehouse	Product			
	1	2	3	4
Buffalo	176	592	1222	858
Atlanta	881	1769	838	670
Dallas	1086	558	1950	734
Denver	647	1131	960	1618

TABLE 15. Facilities: Productive Capacity

Facility	Product			
	1	2	3	4
Gadsden	72	358	1446	816
Springfield	975	2000	336	534
Oxnard	1858	1875	2260	2620

TABLE 16. Transportation Costs (As Percent of Product Cost)

Warehouse	Facility		
	Gadsden	Springfield	Oxnard
Buffalo	.077	.063	.237
Atlanta	.010	.055	.210
Dallas	.066	.069	.139
Denver	.121	.089	.092

To conceptualize the material in our text, a model will be utilized throughout these next chapters. Figure 22 is an example. It delineates the general character of the structured information file and demonstrates the logical relationships between items of information.

There are two categories of records stored within this general characterization. The first is generic categories of information. For example, if one were dealing with four types of information such as (1) products, (2) salesmen, (3)

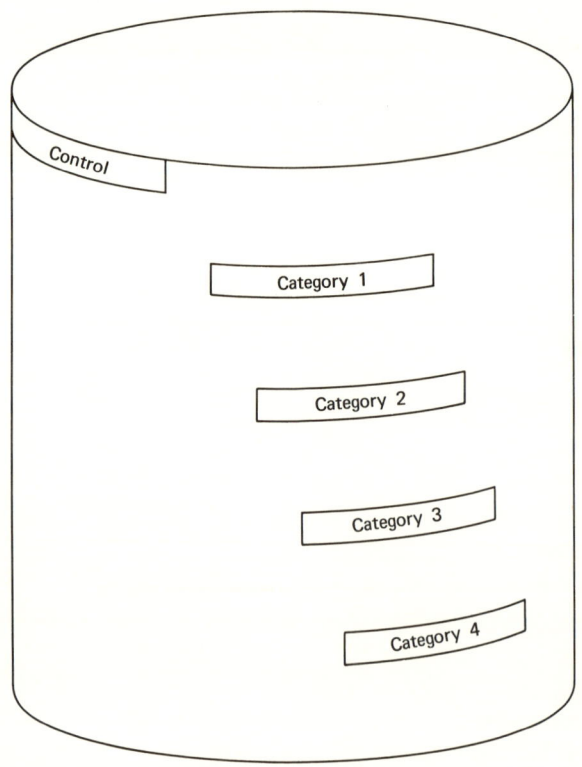

Figure 22. The general character of the structured information file.

warehouses, and (4) facilities; these would be identified as category one, category two, category three, and category four. The second type of information would be a control record of some nature and would include the processor's information to identify data on the file, where it starts, how much there is, and so forth.

C. DEVELOPING THE MODEL

The model we will discuss was developed on an IBM System/360 Model 40 containing two Model 2311 disk drives. We have restricted the structured information file to 400 records. Thus the home addresses are numbered 000 to 399.

The initial requisite for creating the file is to assure that the disk area is clear. A maintenance program is written to perform this housekeeping function. A one is placed in the check character position while the remainder of the record is set to blank.

The file is now available for data entry. These source data are usually converted to punch cards and are entered record by record. Each record is read and

TABLE 17. Records and Generated Home Addresses

Record	Identification Number	Home Address
Salesmen		
Ahling	189975530	312
Beach	870942512	340
Casey	584154882	349
Esslinger	105131174	017
Haupert	269381443	270
Nortmann	393087232	065
Wyjack	797331182	353
Zeithamel	264706850	352
Facilities		
Gadsden	647558103	288
Oxnard	388584025	029
Springfield	122259228	300
Warehouse		
Denver	201769977	286
Dallas	615655436	144
Buffalo	950459344	057
Atlanta	594728038	204
Product		
DH - 15 Tractor	231575485	225
DH - 17 Cotton-Picker	901837259	150
DH - 19 Reaper	376249708	105
DH - 21 Baler	869523036	139

a home address is generated. If the home address locations is free, the basic record is stored there. If it is not free, the next sequential address is examined and if free, the record will be stored. The synonym address linkage will be established in the preceding location of the chain. This develops a model with the five common elements contained in the records. The analysis of entry procedure methods presented earlier proved that the home address can be satisfactorily generated by using the remainder following division by the largest prime number under the record capacity. This technique was incorporated in the structured file model with the prime number of 397. Each record and its home address are shown in Table 17.

Logical relationships between record categories are put in card form. These cards represent the products that each salesman handles, the production plants, the warehouses, and other pertinent information. The required linkages are established as data are stored.

Logical ties are maintained as three digit home address locations rather than using the nine digit identification numbers. As a guiding principle, each item of data will be recorded in only one place in the file. Such items as a salesman's name will be recorded only in the salesman's record and not in the segment of the product record describing who sells that product. That linkage would be accomplished by recording the home address of the particular salesman at some point in the product record. This procedure continues until all data are entered. At that time, the file has been completely established.

D. STRUCTURED INFORMATION FILE

We can now examine the contents of each of the disk record types for this structured information file example.

The record formats are sufficiently linked so that movement throughout the file between record classes as well as among records of the same class is a reality. Five elements are common to each record category: (1) the check character, (2) an identification number, (3) a data overflow link, (4) a category link, and (5) a synonym link. Appropriate data and linkages are established for each of the four record types and are illustrated and explained in the following.

Each product record (see Table 18) contains cost and description information as well as linkages to records of a producing facility, a storing warehouse, and to a salesman responsible for the product. The specific product records and their pertinent data are displayed in Table 19.

Each of the logical linkages is graphically presented. Figure 23 displays the product to producing facility linkage. The product to warehouse linkage is shown in Figure 24 while the product to salesman linkage is shown in Figure 25. Finally, the product to product linkages is presented in Figure 26.

TABLE 18. Product Record

Field	Positions
Check Character (P)	1
Identification Number	2-10
Product Cost	11-17
Production Description	18-37
Bill-of-Materials Link	38-40
Producing Facility Link	41-43
Warehouse Link	44-46
Salesman Link	47-49
Other Information	50-107
Data Overflow	108-110
Category Link	111-113
Synonym	114-116

TABLE 19. Product Disk Records

HA	Cost	Made	Stored	Sold	Description	Cat-Link
225	631987	288	286	132	Tractor	150
150	723476	288	286	312	Cotton-Picker	105
105	918899	288	286	312	Reaper	139
139	1199504	288	286	312	Baler	225

Although not a part of this example, please note that a link into a bill-of-materials file would normally be present and a field has been allocated for that purpose (Figure 27). Stemming from the bill-of-materials linkage an entire file would be available containing routing data and master operation listings that would provide complete information for the construction of the product in a total operating system.

Table 20 includes the field incorporated in the salesman's record. The actual disk records for the model are shown in Table 21. These include linkages and data referencing each product serviced by the salesman (Figure 28). Each product field contains the home address of the product, a category link to another salesman's record (Figure 29), and the quantity of this product sold. These three sections are included for every product handled by the salesman. If more than four products are treated, they fall into additional records, linked by the data overflow address. Figure 30 illustrates the overall salesman to salesman linkage.

Similarly, the facility record contains a sub-field for each product produced and shipping charge schedules to the warehouses. The general character of the facility record is shown in Table 22 while the data for the model appear in Table 23 and 24.

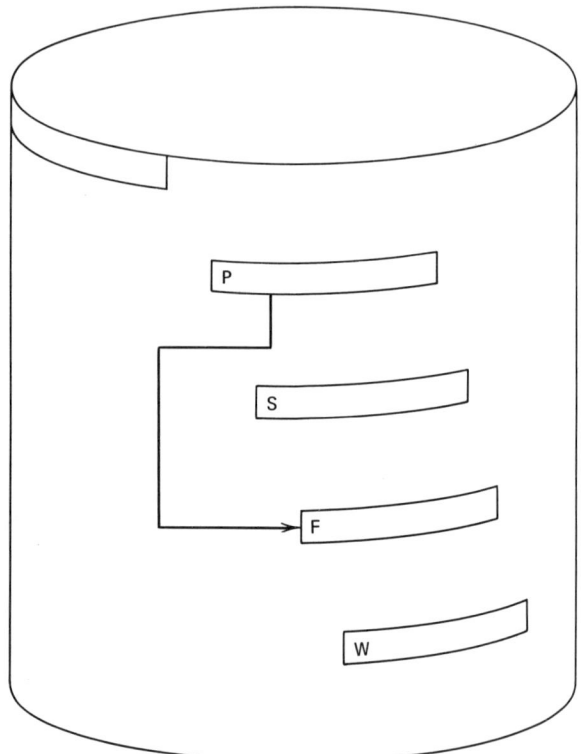

Figure 23. *Product to producing facility linkage.*

The sub-fields included the home address of the product (Figure 31), the product inventory, and the production capacity of the facility. In our example three facilities were involved and thus there was a relatively small number of facilities in comparison with products and salesmen and it was not necessary to provide sublinkages between facilities for each product. The same result was reached using the category link common element and searching the product home address sub-field until the desired segment of the facility record was identified (Figure 32).

Transportation charges are incorporated within the stream of information, by adding two items to the facility record, i.e., the warehouse home address (Figure 33) and the shipping charge to that warehouse as a percentage of product cost.

Each warehouse record in Table 25 contains specific information regarding products stored. Vertical linkages have been established that identify the home address (Figure 34) and two other data items; (1) the quantity on-hand and (2) the quantity required by the warehouse. The overall category link is shown in Figure 35. Table 26 displays the specific contents of the warehouse disk records.

TABLE 20. Salesmen Record

Field	Positions
Check Character (S)	1
Identification Number	2-10
Product 1	
Product home address	11-13
Salesman link	14-16
Quantity sold	17-19
Product 2	
Product home address	20-22
Salesman link	23-25
Quantity sold	26-28
Product 3	
Product home address	29-31
Salesman link	32-34
Quantity sold	35-37
Product 4	
Product home address	38-40
Salesman link	41-43
Quantity sold	44-46
Other Information	47-86
Salesmen names	87-107
Data Overflow	108-110
Category Link	111-113
Synonym	114-116

TABLE 21. Salesmen Disk Records

Home Address	Product Data 1			2			3			4			Name	Cat-Link
	HA	Link	Qty	HA	Link	Qty	HA	Link	Qty	HA	Link	Qty		
312	225	349	74	150	340	74	105	349	10	139	349	38	Ahling	340
340	150	349	97										Beach	349
349	225	270	55	150	17	8	105	17	22	139	17	67	Casey	017
017	150	65	90	105	270	11	139	270	49				Esslinger	270
270	225	65	55	105	65	54	139	65	51				Haupert	065
065	225	353	4	150	353	18	105	352	38	139	353	94	Nortman	353
353	225	352	31	150	352	37	139	312	5				Wyjack	352
352	225	312	3	150	312	44	105	312	34				Zeithamel	312

E. CONTROL RECORDS

The use of a control record is a necessary requirement in any random processing application. The control record coordinates activities within this area of the structured information file. It is usually physically located in an "early" section of the random access unit as shown in Figure 36. Table 27 lists the items

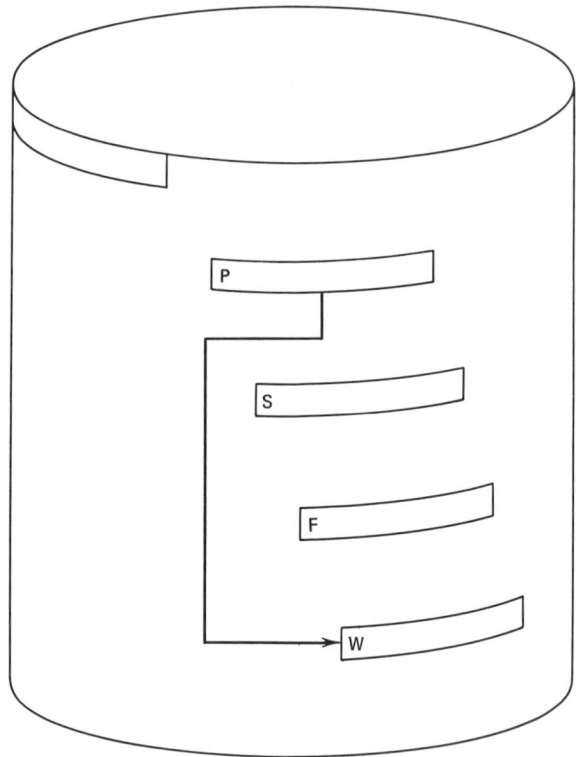

Figure 24. *Product to warehouse linkage.*

that might be part of the control record. The first home address of the product chain is normally one of the items stored. It may be the beginning of an alphabetic chain or a social security ordered sequence, but frequently it is chosen to have some logical meaning rather than just any link in that chain. Secondly, the number of products on the file is maintained. Similarly, the beginning home address of the salesmen chain and the number of salesmen on the file, the beginning home address of the facility chain and the number of facilities, and the beginning home address of the warehouse chain and the number of warehouses on the file are stored. For additional classes of information, similar data would be maintained on each one of them. Frequently the file maintenance date would be useful to retain in this control record. Other items considered for storing in the other data fields might include some indication of the current packing of the random access unit. For example, a historical record could be kept of the growth pattern of the random access unit allowing one adequately to plan moving to a larger or smaller unit.

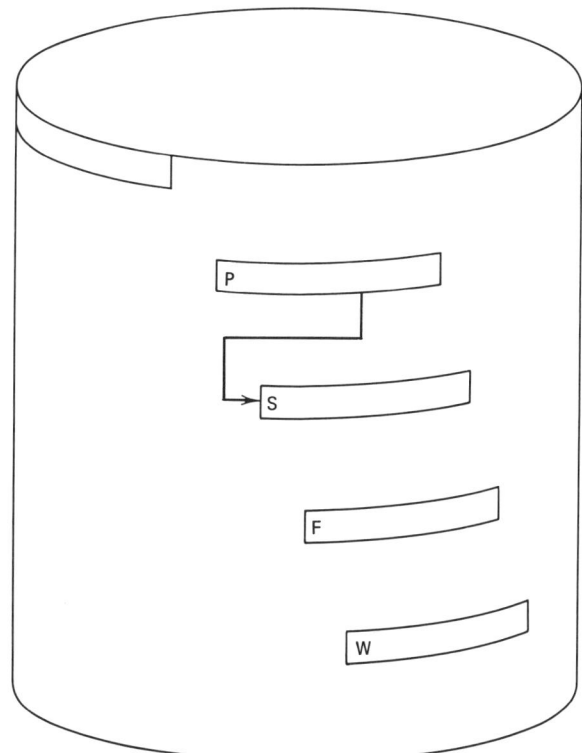

Figure 25. *Product to salesman linkage.*

The completed skeleton of the structured information file for the product salesman facility and warehouse model is shown in Figure 37. As can be seen there are a multitude of linkages and associations possible for rapid and precise communication between all segments of the information file. A completely flexible, structured information file has been demonstrated.

F. REPORT GENERATION

A structured information file must allow ease of use. The following is a demonstration of this quality. Three reports will be developed on the model described in the previous chapters supporting the thesis that the model elements are structured to allow associative date gathering and manipulation.

The first of the three reports reflects a salesman's performance: summary results totaling the quantities sold based on the value for each product each salesman is responsible for selling.

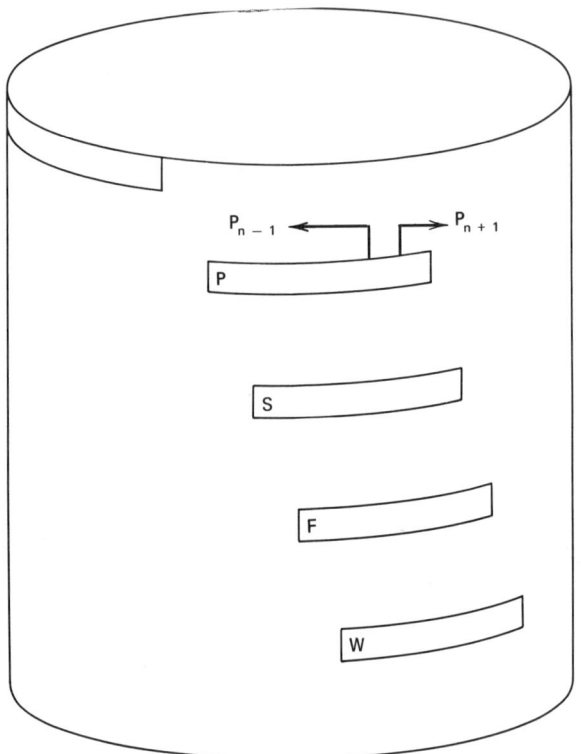

Figure 26. *Product to product linkage.*

The sales analysis report (Table 28) began with the first record in the salesman chain. The product home address in the sub-fields was accessed to extract the product characteristic number and cost. By combining this with the units sold, recorded in the sub-field of the salesman's records, the sales value was calculated. Through successive sub-fields, each product sold could be processed identically. The category linkage provided the next salesman's record and the sales summarization was continued until all sales had been accounted for and a grand total was computed.

This can be summarized as follows. First, access the control record to determine the first salesman. Second, seek and read the first salesman's record. Third, use the product sold sub-field to access the product record to extract the product identification number and unit cost. Fourth, return to the salesman's record to select and access the next product. Fifth, after processing all products sold by this salesman, use the overall category link to seek the next salesman's record. This sequence of steps is shown in Figure 38.

Report Generation 61

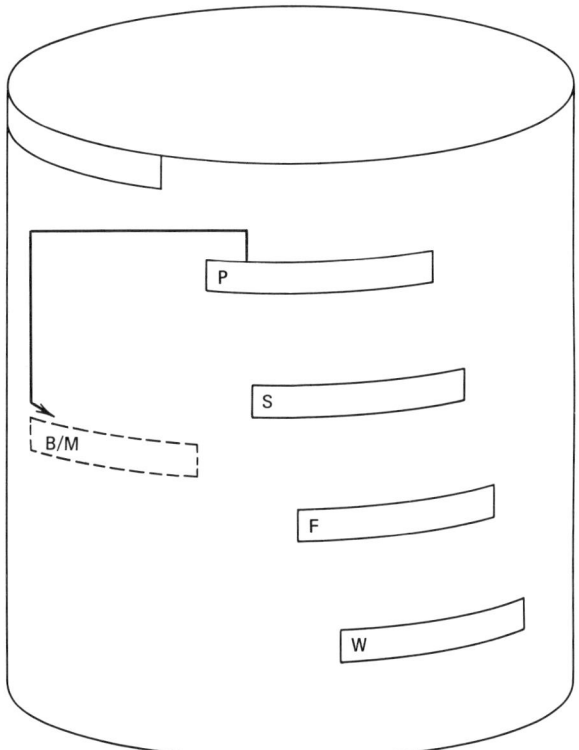

Figure 27. *Product to bill-of-materials linkage.*

The following is a specific example of how the structured information file processes the data for this report. The record for Martin Ahling, home address 312, is accessed extracting the man's name. Examining the product data reveals that the product located at home address 225 has been sold by Ahling, and that he has sold 74 units. The product record at home address 225 is accessed. This product is number 231575485, the DH 15 Tractor with a sales price of $6,319.87. Using the quantity sold from the product sub-field, the total value is merely a simple multiplication.

Continued examination of the product data sub-fields shows that 74 units were also sold of the product located at home address 150. This home address is accessed and found to be product number 901837259, a DH 17 Cotton Picker with a sales price of $7,234.76. The extension of price from the product record and quantity from the salesman's record is performed. When all of the product data associated with Ahling have been accounted, his total sales is printed. The next salesman in the chain is then accessed by examining the category link in

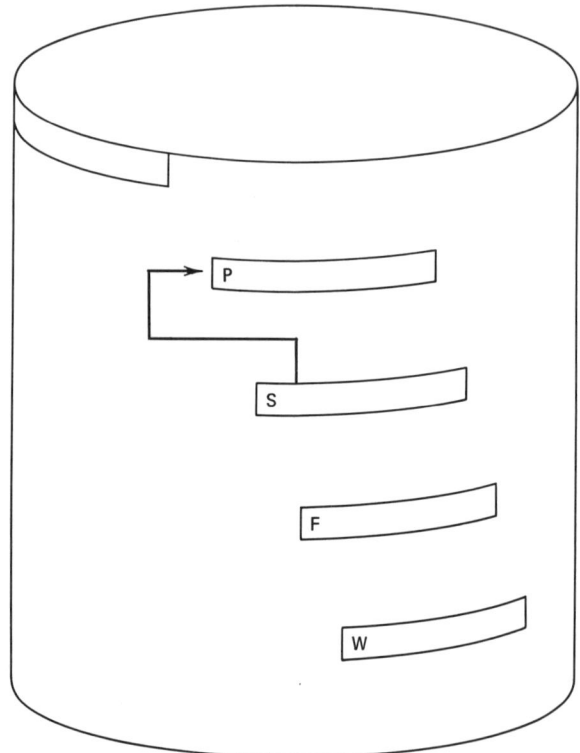

Figure 28. *Product sold by salesman linkage.*

Ahling's record. Home address 340 is found and that record reveals it to be salesman Robert D. Beach. Processing continues as described above. Following the printing of the last salesman's total sales, the grand total of all sales is printed.

The stock status report is the second of the three reports, and is shown in Table 29. It begins at one of the product records and accesses the facility chain through the where-made linkage to determine the nominated product inventory. Utilizing the facility category linkage, each successive producer was examined. The warehouse chain was entered via the where-stored linkage in the product record to complete the status report for each part number. After examining the warehouse record sub-fields for the quantity on-hand of the nominated part number, the warehouse category linkage was utilized to include the other warehouses. The parts inventory status, using the category linkage was repeated with each successive product until all product quantities on-hand were computed.

The specific steps may be summarized as follows. First, the control record

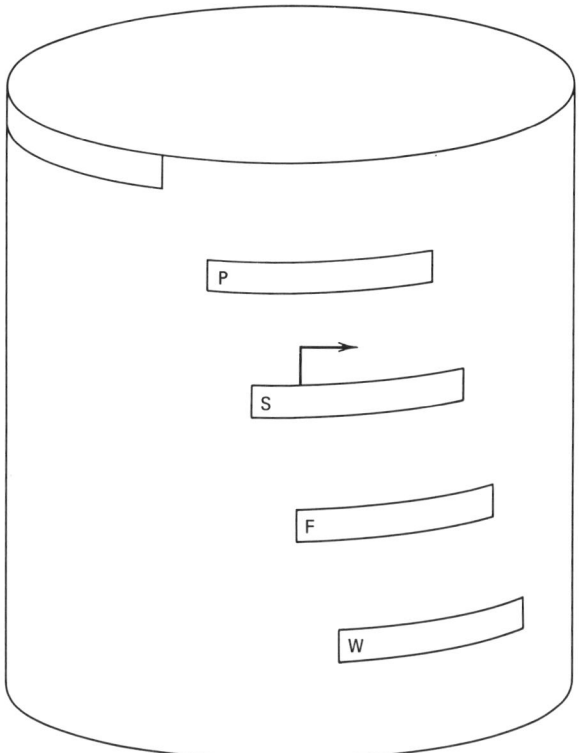

Figure 29. *Salesman to salesman linkage for any given product.*

is accessed to select the first product home address. Second, the first product home record is read. Third, the facility linkage is used to access a factory where this product is made for on-hand inventory data. Fourth, the facility category link is used to access the next factory to determine if the production is on hand there. Fifth, when all facilities have been examined, the product record is again examined to access the first warehouse. Sixth, the warehouse category linkage is used to access the next warehouse. Seventh, when all warehouses have been examined, the product category linkage is used to access the next product. Figure 39 shows these steps.

The third report involves those factors associated with distribution. It is assumed that the ultimate solution to the distribution problem would be through linear programming. Thus, the third report should present the quantities required at each warehouse, the production capabilities of each facility, and the transportation costs of each facility-warehouse combination. This report must be prepared for each product. The resulting reports for our example are shown in

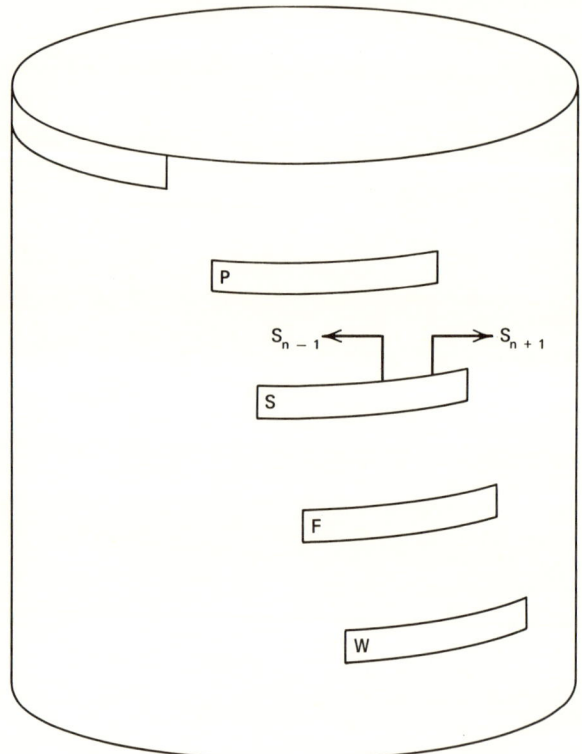

Figure 30. *Salesman to salesman linkage.*

Tables 30 to 33. The data in these tables are in the form suitable for input into a linear programming solution for least-cost transportation decision making. These tables and the associated logic that created them support the value of accessibility to logically related files of information.

Beginning with the first product produced in a facility record, the product cost was extracted and multiplied by the shipping charge factor in the warehouse segment of the record. Each subsequent facility was then accessed via the category linkage and the procedure repeated until the transportation charges matrix was completed. The requirements and capacities were extracted from the warehouse and facilities records respectively. After completing the report for the first product, the original facility record was accessed to begin preparation of the shipping charges matrix for the second product and succeeding products until the total transportation charges had been determined.

Once again the summary of the steps taken are as follows. First, the control record is accessed. Second, attention is directed to the first facility.

TABLE 22. Facility Record

Field	Positions
Check Character (F)	1
Identification Number	2-10
Product 1	
Product home address	11-13
Quantity on-hand	14-17
Capacity	18-21
Product 2	
Product home address	22-24
Quantity on-hand	25-28
Capacity	29-32
Product 3	
Product home address	33-35
Quantity on-hand	36-39
Capacity	40-43
Product 4	
Product home address	44-46
Quantity on-hand	47-50
Capacity	51-54
Shipping Charges (% of product cost)	
To warehouse 1	
warehouse home address	55-57
shipping charge	58-60
To warehouse 2	
warehouse home address	61-63
shipping charge	64-66
To warehouse 3	
warehouse home address	67-69
shipping charge	70-72
To warehouse 4	
warehouse home address	73-75
shipping charge	76-78
Facility Location	79-107
Data Overflow	108-110
Category Link	111-113
Synonym	114-116

TABLE 23. Facility Records—Product Data

Home Address	Product Data 1			2			3			4			Location	Cat-Link
	HA	OH	Cap	HA	OH	Cap	HA	OH	Cap	HA	OH	Cap		
288	225	24	72	150	119	358	105	482	1446	139	272	816	Gadsden	029
029	225	627	1858	150	625	1875	105	755	2260	139	874	2620	Oxnard	300
300	225	325	975	150	667	2000	105	112	336	139	178	534	Springfield	288

Moving About Within the File

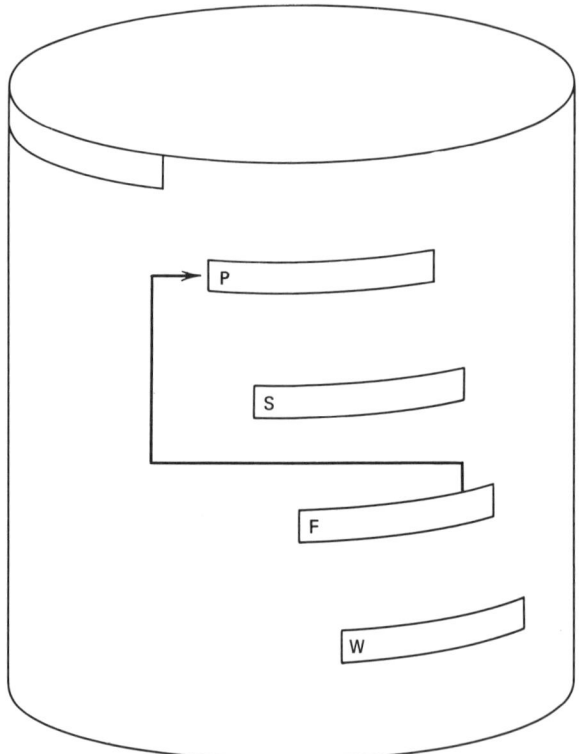

Figure 31. *Product made by facility linkage.*

TABLE 24. Facility Records—Warehouse Shipping Data

	Warehouse Data									
	1		2		3		4			Cat-
HA	Wh	Cost	Wh	Cost	Wh	Cost	Wh	Cost	Location	Link
288	57	077	204	010	144	066	286	121	Gadsden	029
029	57	237	204	210	144	139	286	092	Oxnard	300
300	57	063	204	055	144	069	286	089	Springfield	288

Third, the product record is accessed to extract cost. Fourth, the warehouse record is accessed to extract the percentage shipping charge. Fifth, the warehouse category linkage is used to extract percentage shipping charges from each successive warehouse. Sixth, the facility category linkage is used to incorporate

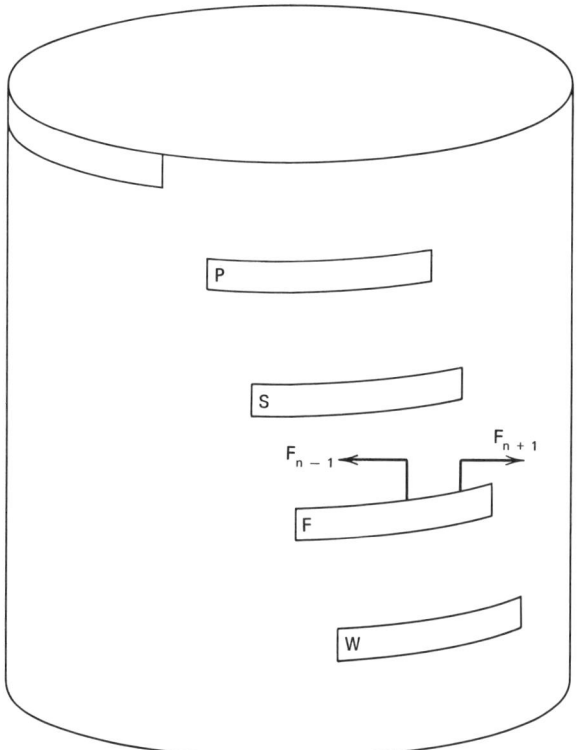

Figure 32. *Facility to facility linkage.*

the next facility. Seventh, the product matrix is complete, the next product is analyzed by returning to the facility record and accessing the next product produced. These steps are shown in Figure 40.

These three reports validate the structural accuracy of the structured information file concept. It works and provides accessibility to multiple level or multiple category records.

Although the file demonstrated in this example is not of major size, this is not an important factor. The logic that holds for linking multiple levels of records with multiple items of information within each class is consistent whether there are four classes of information or four hundred and whether there are four items within each class or hundred of thousands within each class. The logic remains the same; the chain linking concept holds.

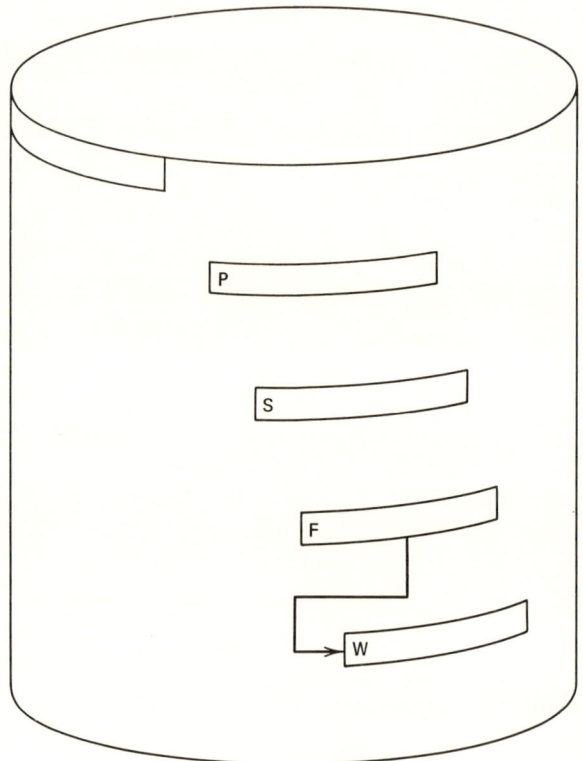

Figure 33.   *Facility to warehouse linkage.*

G. SUMMARY

We have discussed the internal linkages required to move about within the file in an efficient manner. Five elements are suggested as common to each record type in the structured information file. Details concerning a production distribution system and sample data for test purposes are presented. A complete model of the system is demonstrated that totally integrates the record categories.

By applying data from the model the use of the structured information file is clear. A variety of reports are developed that draw upon data found in separate categories. Yet the data are recorded in one place.

Summary   69

TABLE 25. Warehouse Record

Field	Positions
Check Character (W)	1
Identification Number	2-10
Product 1	
Product home address	11-13
Quantity on-hand	14-17
Quantity required	18-21
Product 2	
Product home address	22-24
Quantity on-hand	25-28
Quantity required	29-32
Product 3	
Product home address	33-35
Quantity on-hand	36-39
Quantity required	40-43
Product 4	
Product home address	44-46
Quantity on-hand	47-50
Quantity required	51-54
Other Information	55-87
Warehouse Location	88-107
Data Overflow	108-110
Category Link	111-113
Synonym	114-116

TABLE 26. Warehouse Disk Records

| | Product Data | | | | | | | | | | | |
| | 1 | | | 2 | | | 3 | | | 4 | | | | Cat- |
HA	HA	OH	Req	HA	OH	Req	HA	OH	Req	HA	OH	Req	Location	Link
286	225	82	647	150	296	1131	105	216	960	139	14	1618	Denver	144
144	225	31	1086	150	77	558	105	87	1950	139	110	734	Dallas	59
059	225	99	176	150	65	592	105	21	1222	139	93	858	Buffalo	204
204	225	98	881	150	12	1769	105	106	838	139	203	670	Atlanta	286

70 *Moving About Within the File*

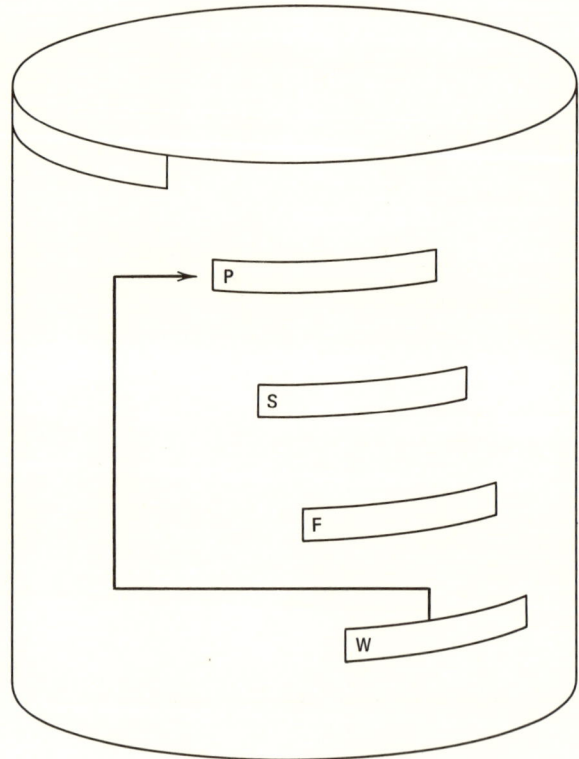

Figure 34. *Product stored by warehouse linkage.*

TABLE 27. The Control Record

Item
Check Character (X)
Beginning home address of product chain Number of products on the file
Beginning home address of salesman chain Number of salesmen on the file
Beginning home address of facility chain Number of facilities on the file
Beginning home address of warehouse chain Number of warehouses on the file
Date of latest file maintenance
Other data

TABLE 28. Sales Analyses

Name	Product No.	Units	Value	Total
Ahling, Martin	231575485	74	$ 467,670.38	
	901837259	74	535,372.24	
	376249708	10	91,889.90	
	869523036	38	455,811.52	
				$ 1,550,744.04
Beach, Robert D.	901837259	97	701,771.72	
				701,771.72
Casey, Bernard	231575485	55	347,592.85	
	901837259	08	57,878.08	
	376249708	22	202,157.78	
	896523036	67	803,667.68	
				1,411,296.39
Esslinger, William	901837259	90	651,128.40	
	376249708	11	101,078.89	
	869523036	49	587,756.96	
				1,339,964.25
Haupert, Raymond B.	231575485	55	347,592.85	
	376249708	54	496,205.46	
	869523036	51	611,747.04	
				1,455,545.35
Nortmann, George B.	231575485	04	25,279.48	
	901837259	18	130,225.68	
	376249708	38	349,181.62	
	869523036	94	1,127,533.76	
				1,632,220.54
Wyjack, Harvey	231575485	31	195,915.97	
	901837259	37	267,686.12	
	869523036	05	59,975.20	
				523,577.29
Zeithamel, William L.	231575485	03	18,959.61	
	901837259	44	318,329.44	
	376249708	34	312,425.66	
				649,714.71
Grand Total				$ 9,264,834.29

TABLE 29. Stock Status—Quantities On-Hand

Product	Description	Location	Units
231575485	DH - 15 Tractor	Gadsden, Ala.	24
		Oxnard, Calif.	627
		Springfield, Mo.	325
		Denver, Colo.	82
		Dallas, Tex.	31
		Buffalo, N. Y.	99
		Atlanta, Ga.	98
		Total	1,286
901837259	DH - 17 Cotton Picker	Gadsden, Ala.	119
		Oxnard, Calif.	625
		Springfield, Mo.	667
		Denver, Colo.	296
		Dallas, Tex.	77
		Buffalo, N. Y.	65
		Atlanta, Ga.	12
		Total	1,861
376249708	DH - 19 Reaper	Gadsden, Ala.	482
		Oxnard, Calif.	755
		Springfield, Mo.	112
		Denver, Colo.	216
		Dallas, Tex.	87
		Buffalo, N. Y.	21
		Atlanta, Ga.	106
		Total	1,779
869523036	DH - 21 Baler	Gadsden, Ala.	272
		Oxnard, Calif.	874
		Springfield, Mo.	178
		Denver, Colo.	14
		Dallas, Tex.	110
		Buffalo, N. Y.	93
		Atlanta, Ga.	203
		Total	1,744

Summary

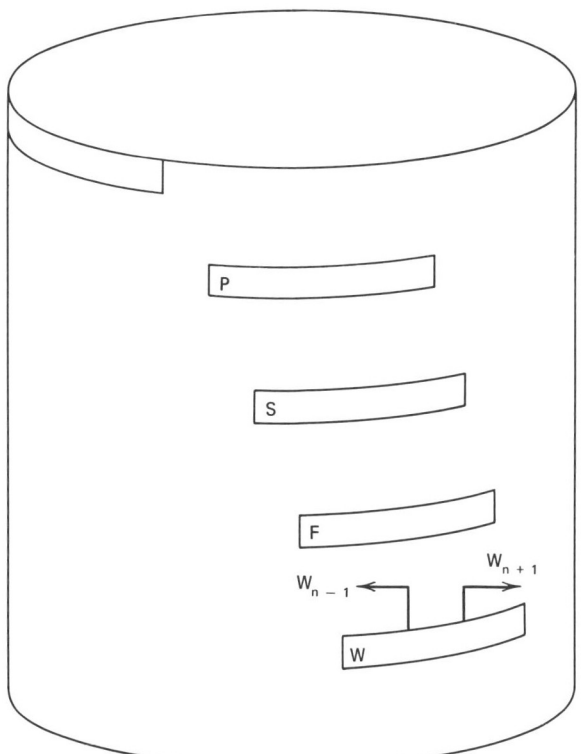

Figure 35. *Warehouse to warehouse linkage.*

TABLE 30. Transportation Costs: DH - 15 Tractor

	Gadsden	Oxnard	Springfield	Requirements
Buffalo	$486.62	$1,497.80	$398.15	176
Atlanta	$ 63.19	$1,327.17	$347.59	881
Denver	$417.11	$ 878.46	$436.07	647
Dallas	$764.70	$ 581.42	$562.46	1086
Capacity	72	1,858	975	2905 2790

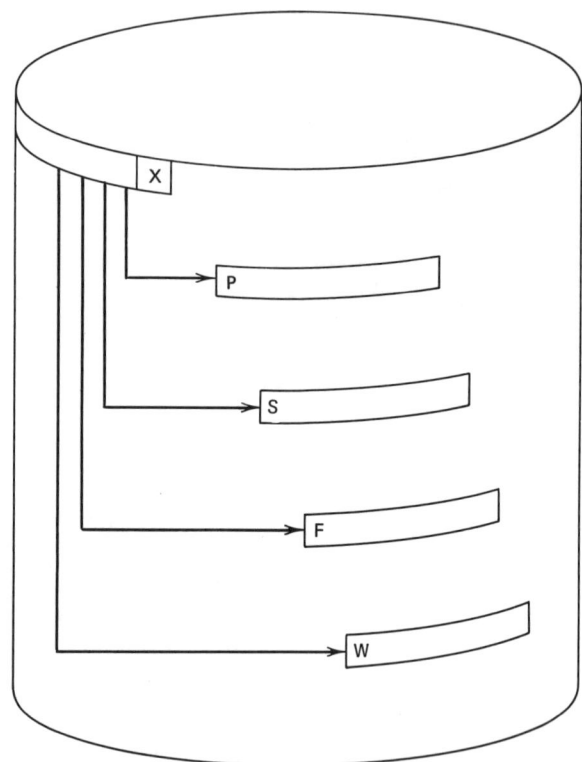

Figure 36. *The control record.*

TABLE 31. Transportation Costs: DH - 17 Cotton Picker

	Gadsden	Oxnard	Springfield	Requirements
Buffalo	$557.07	$1,714.63	$455.78	592
Atlanta	$ 72.34	$1,519.29	$397.91	1769
Denver	$477.49	$1,005.63	$499.19	1131
Dallas	$875.40	$ 665.59	$643.89	558 4050
Capacity	358	1,875	2,000	4233

Summary 75

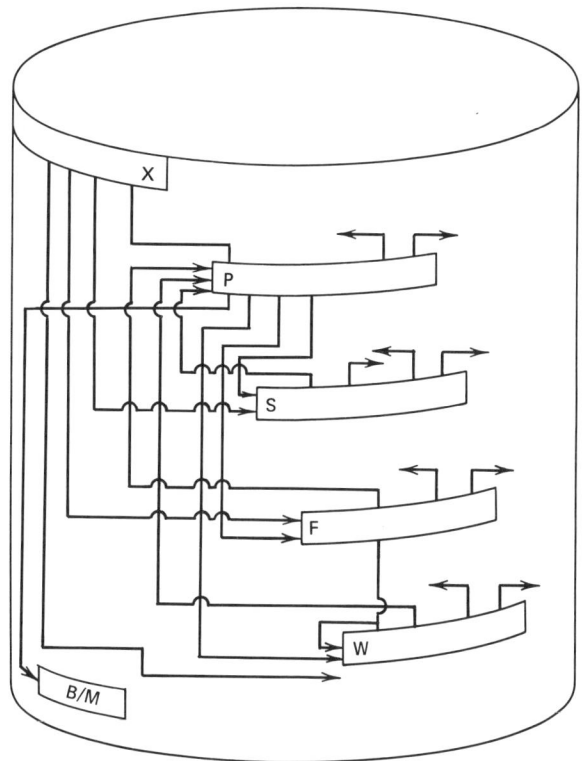

Figure 37. *Complete skeleton structured file for the product, salesman, facility, and warehouse model.*

TABLE 32. Transportation Costs: DH - 19 Reaper

	Gadsden	Oxnard	Springfield	Requirements
Buffalo	$ 707.55	$2,177.79	$578.90	1222
Atlanta	$ 91.88	$1,929.68	$505.39	838
Denver	$ 606.47	$1,277.26	$634.04	920
Dallas	$1,111.86	$ 845.38	$817.38	1950 4970
Capacity	1,446	2,260	336	4042

Moving About Within the File

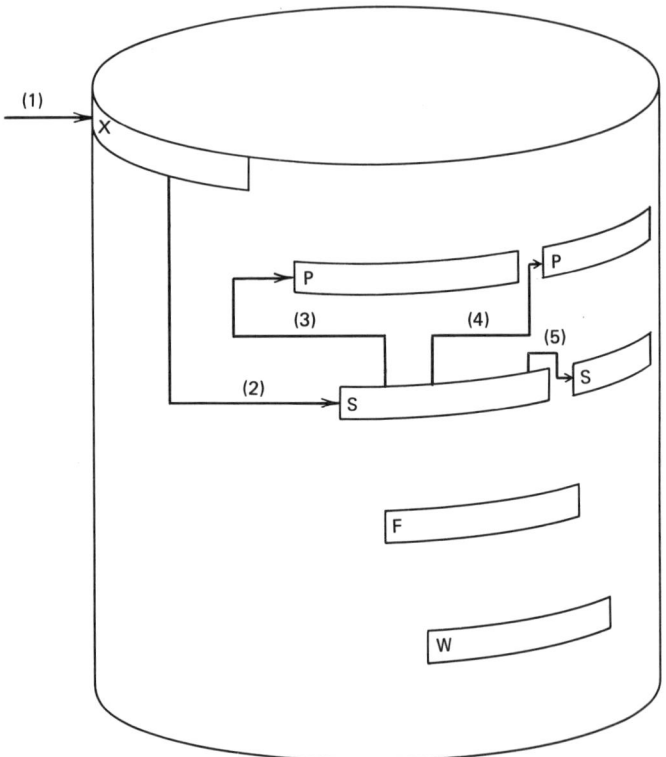

Figure 38. *Preparing the sales report.*

TABLE 33. Transportation Costs: DH - 21 Baler

	Gadsden	Oxnard	Springfield	Requirements
Buffalo	$ 923.61	$2,842.82	$ 755.68	858
Atlanta	$ 119.95	$2,518.95	$ 659.72	658
Denver	$ 791.67	$1,667.31	$ 827.65	1618
Dallas	$1,451.39	$1,103.54	$1,067.55	734
Capacity	816	2,620	534	3970 3868

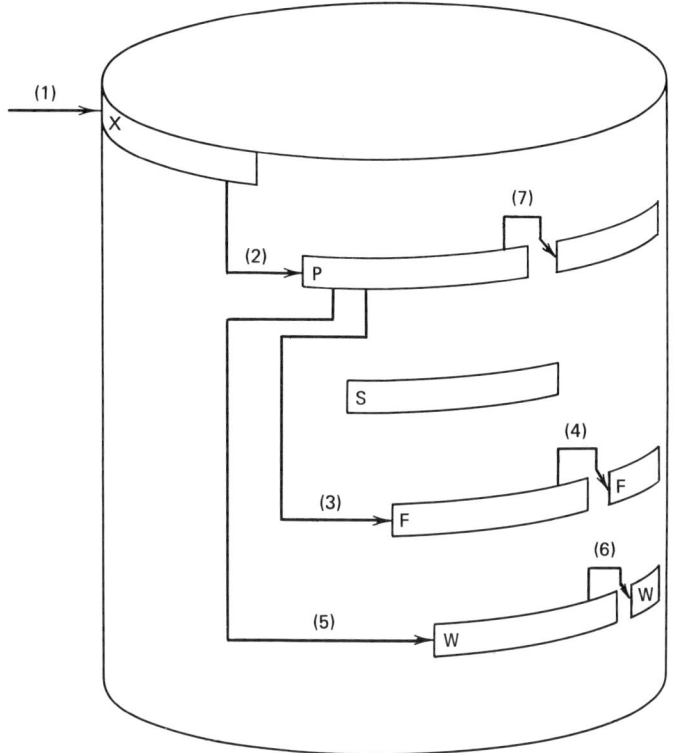

Figure 39. *Preparing the stock status report.*

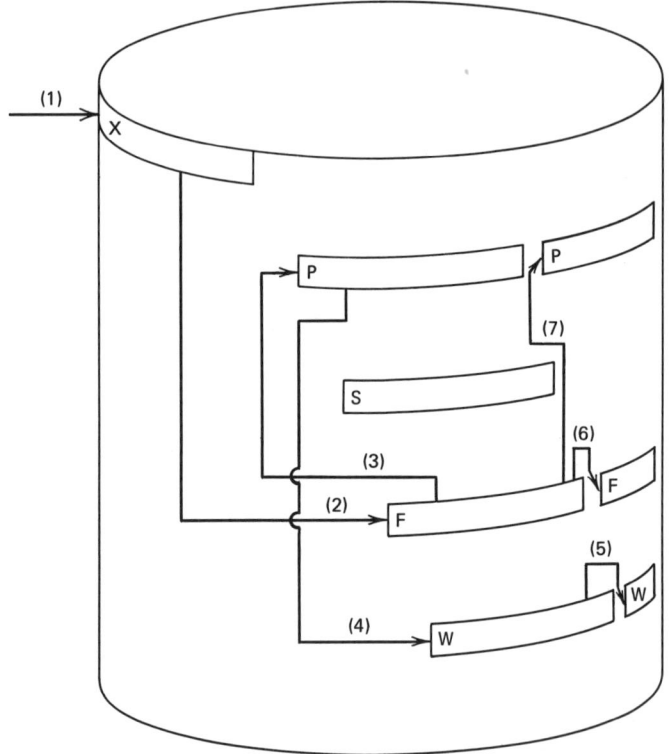

Figure 40. *Preparing the transportation cost matrix.*

Five

Other Considerations

There are a number of aspects of structured information files that have not been discussed. These are:

A. Record placement within the file
B. Organizing by frequency of occurrence
C. File maintenance
D. The need for a retrieval language.

A. RECORD PLACEMENT WITHIN THE FILE

When using a structured information file in an operating environment, it is valuable to determine an optimum placement of records either as they relate to each other through synonyms or other logical linkages. This placement consideration produces a more efficient operation within the frame of reference of the computer.

Operating advantages develop by placing logically related records so that the access arms containing the read-write heads have a minimum distance to travel. For example, if Record A was linked to Record B, no arm movement would be required if the two records were either located on the same track or located within the same cylinder. It is highly desirable to minimize the arm travel because it is the mechanical movement of the arms rather than the electronic transfer of data that causes a bottleneck.

Figure 41 illustrates the concept of relating logical records A and B by a physical relationship. As described earlier, each of the platters would have an access arm with a read-write head associated with it to perform to input-output functions. Thus a request for records A and B would mean zero arm movement if they are linked together. The rotation of the platters coupled with the position of the arms form a cylinder of information. The only delay in logically moving from record A to record B would be the latency or the delay of the platter to rotate under the read head of the unit.

To accomplish a minimum of arm travel requires a thorough knowledge of the characteristics of the data use. Awareness of the frequencies of nomination of particular records and their associations to the data records of other classes can not usually be determined when the original file is constructed. As experience is gained with the use of the file, the data should be periodically reorganized and items relocated for greater operating efficiencies.

The efficiency of the file can also be affected by the sequence in which particular operations are performed. If the synonym is assigned immediately upon demand, the first record available will be selected. Should an identification number be introduced following this process it might randomize to the same free record that was just assigned to the synonym. To assure that this inefficient practice does not occur, it would be necessary to randomize and set aside all zero synonym records and the first records of each synonym chain prior

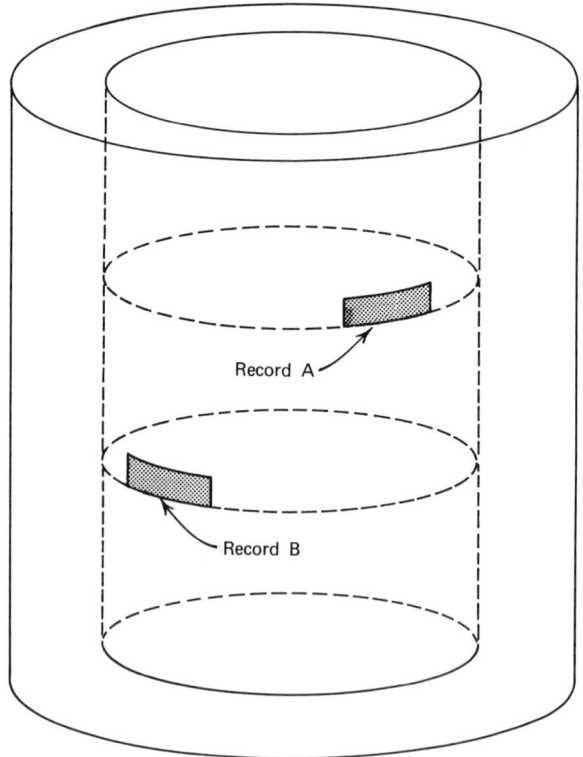

Figure 41.   *The cylinder concept.*

to any synonym linkages. By following this process, each chain of synonyms would be as short as possible and would represent only one original home address. If, on the other hand, the synonyms were assigned as they develop, unnecessary records could be introduced into a synonym chain that represents more than one original home address.

B. ORGANIZING BY FREQUENCY OF OCCURRENCE

The frequency with which records are used might dictate an organization of a category by some scheme other than alphabetic or numeric. This might possibly occur either in the category linkages, e.g., salesmen linked alphabetically or in the synonym linkages. For example, a chain of records that randomize to the same home address would be linked together by the synonyms. If certain records were utilized more frequently than others in this chain, it would be appropriate to place the higher utilized records at the beginning of the chain and the less frequently used records toward the end of the synonym chain.

The question of whether to logically structure items within the categories is demonstrated in Tables 34, 35, and 36. In Table 34 the warehouse list is shown without structure. Thus, Buffalo, Atlanta, Dallas, and Denver merely occur in some random pattern. Associated with each warehouse is a frequency of occurrence of inquiry, and this would indicate that Denver is the busiest in terms of number of inquiries, followed by Buffalo. Of three possible structures, i.e., random, alphabetic, or by frequency of occurrence, the first is undoubtedly the poorest choice in this instance.

Table 35 lists the warehouses, in alphabetical order. If a great number of reports are to be prepared in alphabetic sequence, then this method might be selected.

However, Table 36 seems to offer the greatest opportunity for savings in expensive computer time. The data reveal that the warehouses have a very differing pattern of frequency of inquiry, and it would substantially improve the efficiency of the file if the warehouses were chained in a frequency of occurrence pattern. In effect there would be less synonyms to process in real searches.

C. FILE MAINTENANCE

One major difficulty of information file processing is up-dating for file maintenance. A structured information file with random accessibility offers significant advantages in up-dating informational items within the descriptive fields of a record category. The problem of up-dating and maintaining file linkages is more difficult. The following simplified example demonstrates the logic involved in adding to or deleting a record from a chain.

Other Considerations

TABLE 34. Warehouse List Without Structure

Warehouse Location	Frequency of Inquiry (%)
Buffalo	32
Atlanta	15
Dallas	9
Denver	44

TABLE 35. Warehouse List Alpha Structured

Warehouse Location	Frequency of Inquiry (%)
Atlanta	15
Buffalo	32
Dallas	9
Denver	44

TABLE 36. Warehouse List Frequency of Occurrence Structured

Warehouse Location	Frequency of Inquiry (%)
Denver	44
Buffalo	32
Atlanta	15
Dallas	9

TABLE 37. Warehouses Structured by Frequency of Inquiry with Addresses

Warehouse Location	Home Address	Frequency of Inquiry	Next Warehouse Home Address
Denver	286	44	057
Buffalo	057	32	144
Atlanta	204	15	286
Dallas	144	9	204

Table 37 is a warehouse structure by frequency of inquiry with actual addresses and Figure 42 shows these logically linked warehouses in a chain. Assume that the Dallas warehouse has been suggested by management for elimination. Since it only has a 9 percent frequency of inquiry, management decides that it is too expensive to maintain this additional warehouse; and must remove it from the warehouse chain. Table 38 is an updated warehouse list by frequency of inquiry with the addresses and the Dallas warehouse eliminated. This requires a break in the chain which is logically shown in Figure 43.

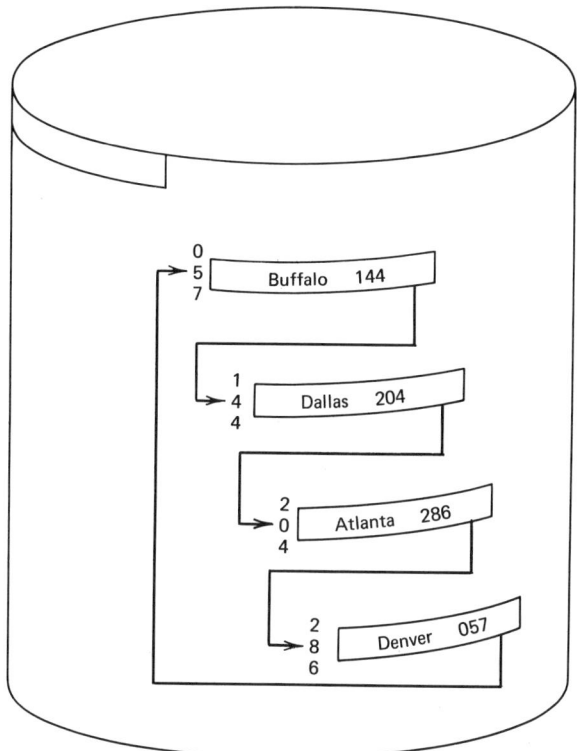

Figure 42. *The logically linked warehouse chain.*

TABLE 38. Updated Warehouses Structured by Frequency of Inquiry with Addresses

Warehouse Location	Home Address	Frequency of Inquiry (%)	Next Warehouse Home Address
Denver	286	44	057
Buffalo	057	32	204
Atlanta	204	15	286

It is necessary to break the tie that had previously linked Buffalo to Dallas and Dallas to Atlanta and substitute a link that ties Buffalo to Atlanta. The three warehouse chain is again complete—Buffalo to Atlanta, Atlanta to Denver, Denver end-linked to Buffalo.

The addition of a new warehouse would be introduced in precisely the same manner. The complexity of any file will add certain logic difficulties to the

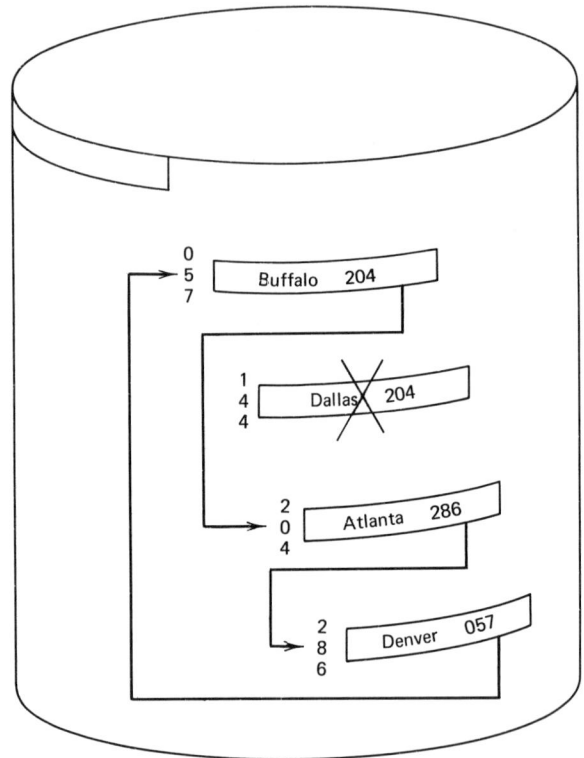

Figure 43. *The logically linked warehouse chain updated.*

file maintenance programming procedures. However, logic is consistent and merely requires care in the preparation of the maintenance program. Maintenance is not a problem. In fact, it may be one of the more difficult procedures in the implementation of a structured information file. However, as this brief discussion indicates, by detailed preparation it can be approached.

D. THE NEED FOR A RETRIEVAL LANGUAGE

Retrieval of data for operational control is a two-pronged problem. First, it involves the design and development of the bank of information in such a manner that logical relationships are maintained between and among subsets of the data. The second is the need for a language for rapid retrieval of any combination of the data to meet the requirements. In an operational control environment the time involved is often a matter of minutes or less. Therefore, the two parts of the data retrieval problem are inseparably interdependent if real-time retrieval is to become a reality.

A structured information file philosophy as has been described in this book will provide an answer to the first part of the problem. Common elements are identified and a general record format is designed containing data and subfield logical linkages.

For the second aspect of the dual problem associated with the large scale automated information system, system designers must develop languages for the actual retrieval of information from the file. The language must allow writing retrieval requests quickly and easily by management personnel with a minimum of computer background.

Reports for this study were prepared by a single purpose program designed to produce a given set of facts and would not be satisfactory for immediate retrieval needs. Further work is necessary to develop inputs to the structured file that reduce response time to a minimum.

Most current medium and large scale computers utilize remote consoles linked to the central processing unit. Future operating managers will likely have console units on their desks and as administrators, rather than data processors, will need a procedural and English-like inquiry language. For example, an operating manager might request the status of a given part number by entering the part number itself and the word "status" on a console seeking only the data in the record for that part number. Since the quantities on-hand in the structured file of this study are stored in the facility, and warehouse records, they would not be retrieved. Thus a thorough interrogation is necessary for in-depth or multiple level searching. Each designer of an management information file for random access must consider the retrieval procedure as well as the file structure.

E. SUMMARY

In this chapter, four considerations concerning the structured information files were discussed. The first examined optimizing the placement of the individual records on the file. The second discussed the potential benefits of linking the records by frequency of occurrence rather than alphabetically or otherwise and the third concerned file maintenance. Finally, the fourth consideration established the need for a retrieval language. It is important to create optimum entry and linkage functions, but it is just as important to be able to retrieve from the file. This requirement requires the creation of a language designed for use by nontechnical management personnel.

Six

Additional Structured Information File Applications

The structured information file has been described thus far with a manufacturing-distribution application as a base. Naturally other fields than business administration might be served by the file scheme by utilizing the five common elements of the records and re-formatting as appropriate. Two such applications are outlined in this section. One additional use of the concept, for processing large tape files, is described.

A. THE STRUCTURED INFORMATION FILE
   IN EDUCATIONAL ADMINISTRATION

Data files can be structured for an educational bank of information.[1] Four basic record types can be identified: (1) pupils, (2) teachers, (3) courses, and (4) schools. The purpose of each record and a suggested description are described in the following.

---

[1] The writer gratefully acknowledges the permission granted by the Automated Education Center to reproduce this material that originally appeared under his name as "Project TUHL: As Integrated Educational Data Bank," *Automated Education Handbook* (Detroit, Michigan: Automated Education Center, 1965), pp. VI A 23-31.

The student record would maintain the ties to relating the student to all other students and to the courses being taken. Included are:

1. The check character (P) identifying the record type.
2. The unique number assigned to each student.
3. Demographic and other information.
4. Curriculum information for courses 1, 2, ... n.
   a. The course home address. (Figure 44).
   b. The grades that the student received and the date that the course was taken.
   c. The front tie relating to the succeeding student enrolled in the course (Figure 45).
5. Data overflow address.
6. Category linkage (Figure 46).
7. Synonym linkage.

The curriculum record relates a course to all other courses, and ties the course to a school, a teacher(s), and the student enrolled in the course. Included are:

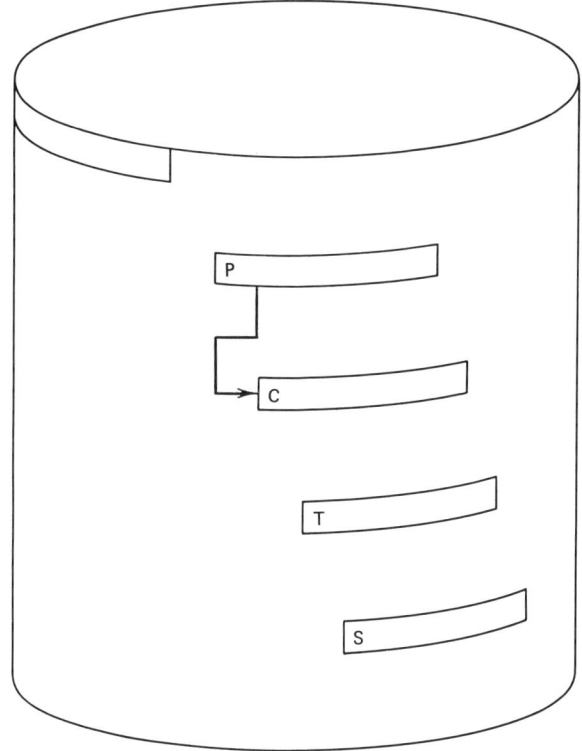

Figure 44. *Pupil to course taken linkage.*

88   *Additional Structured Information File Applications*

1. The check character (C) identifying the type of record.
2. The unique number assigned to each course in each school.
3. Description and content of the course.
4. The home address of the instructor who teaches this course.(Figure 47)
5. The home address of the school in which this course is offered. (Figure 48)
6. The home address of a student enrolled in the course. (Figure 49)
7. Data overflow address.
8. Category linkage (Figure 50)
9. Synonym linkage.

The teacher record relates this teacher to all other teachers, and to the courses taught. Included are:

1. The check character (T) identifying the type of record.
2. The unique number assigned to the teacher.
3. Descriptive and qualifications data pertaining to the teacher.
4. Courses taught ties that will identify the home addresses of the

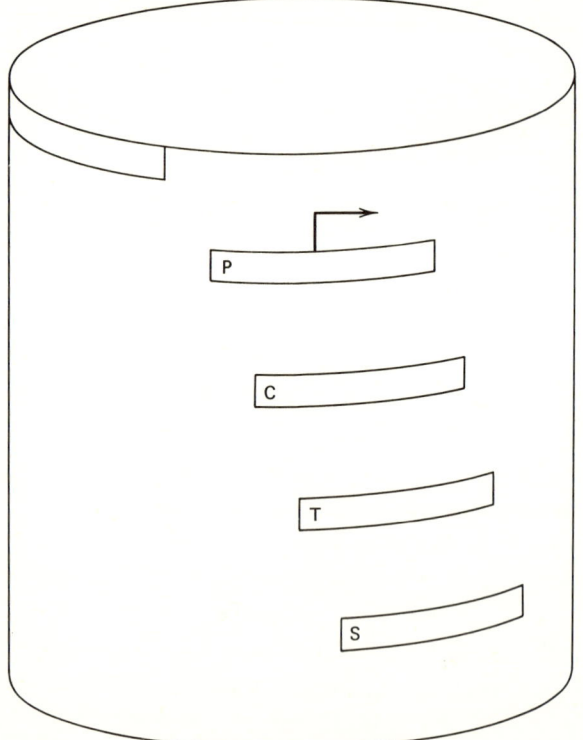

Figure 45.   *Pupil to another pupil enrolled in same course linkage.*

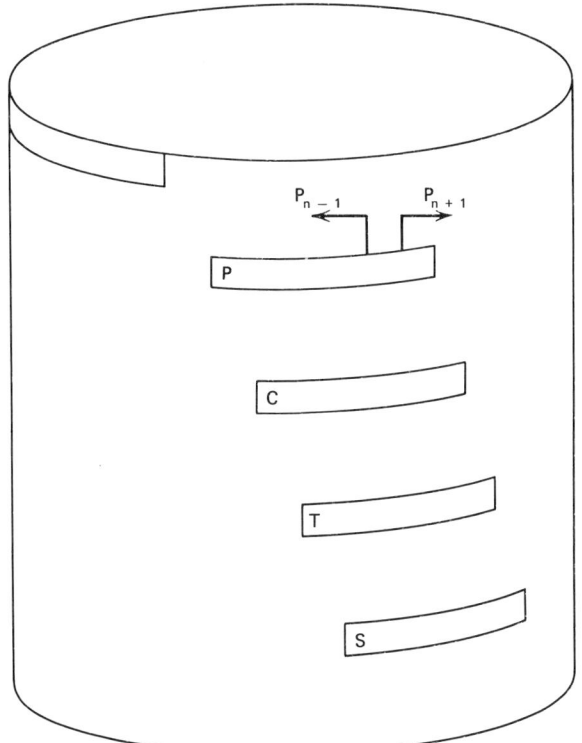

Figure 46. *Pupil to pupil category linkage.*

courses for which this teacher is responsible. (Figure 51)
5. Data overflow address.
6. Category linkage. (Figure 52)
7. Synonym linkage.

The school record relates this school to all other schools and to other pertinent records within the school. Included are:

1. The check character (S) identifying the record type.
2. The unique number assigned to the school.
3. Descriptive information about the school.
4. The home address of a course offered in the school. (Figure 53)
5. Data overflow address.
6. Category linkage. (Figure 54)
7. Synonym linkage.

A school's information maintained in this form offers on-line data for guidance, counseling, attendance reporting, and longitudinal studies. The maintenance of similar data on tape files removes the information from immediate

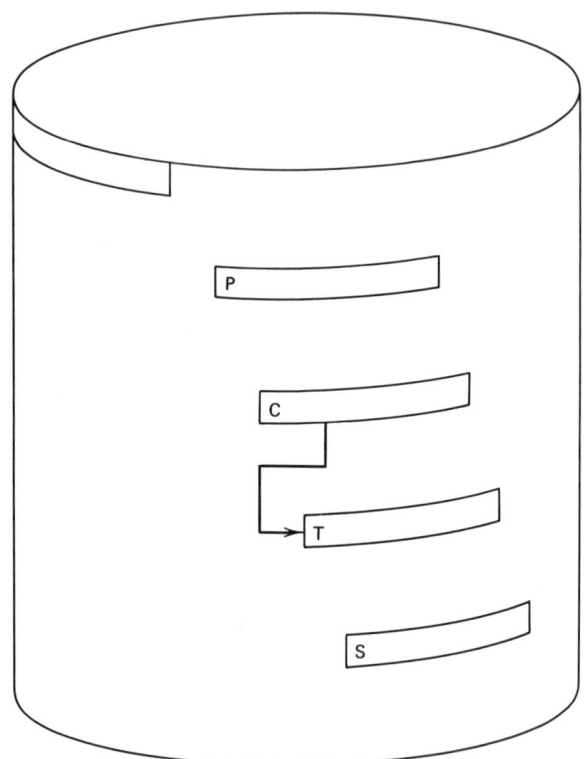

Figure 47. *Course to administering teacher linkage.*

retrieval and substantially complicates research relating to these classes of data. Figure 55 represents an educational structured information file in its conceptual form.

In the following, two typical applications are processed to demonstrate the usefulness of the structured information file for educational purposes.

An instructor calls in sick causing the administrators to require a list of all students taught by that teacher. The structured information file permits the retrieval of these data in a routine manner. Let us examine how this could be done. First, the identification number of the teacher is randomized to gain access to the teacher's record. Second, the teacher's record is examined to learn the first course he teaches. Third, this record is accessed for the names of the pupils enrolled in this course. Fourth, the pupil record is examined for other students in the same course, continuing until all students in this course are identified. Fifth, the teacher record is again referenced to process the second course taught and the above procedure repeated. The steps are described in Figure 56.

A second application might be the preparation of report cards. Initially the control is read which determines the first student in the file. This record

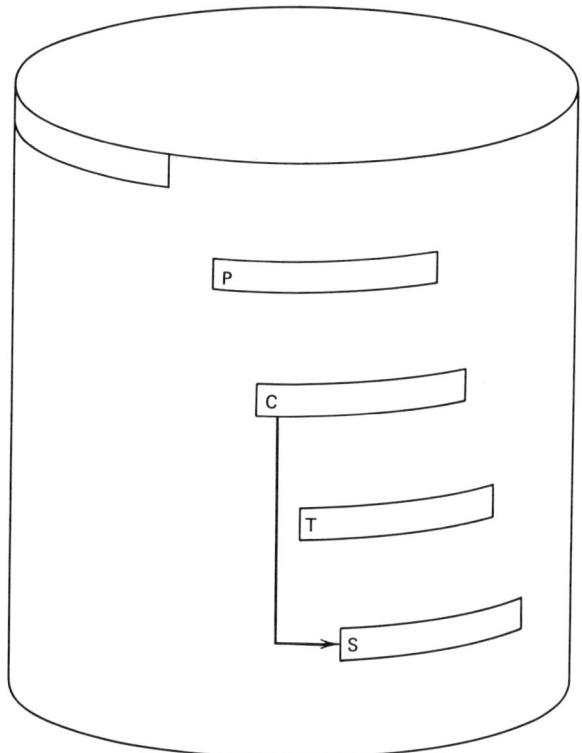

Figure 48. *Course to school in which course is offered linkage.*

identifies the chosen fields of study of the pupil and permits the course name to be identified. The course record references the teacher record and the teacher name. The next course in the pupil record is examined as above until all courses have been examined. Finally the overall category linkage is utilized to read the next student and the procedure repeated. The steps are shown in Figure 57.

B. THE STRUCTURED INFORMATION IN HOSPITAL ADMINISTRATION

Hospital administration offers an additional application of the structured information file. As a basic classification, four types of records can be identified: (1) patients, (2) doctors, (3) drugs, and (4) facilities.

The patient record identifies the patient and maintains the ties to other pertinent records. Contained within the patient record would be the following:

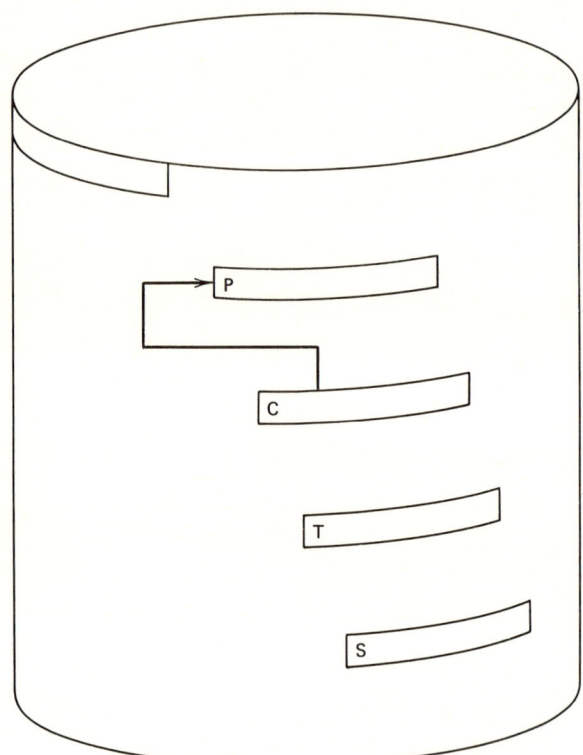

Figure 49. *Course to an enrolled student linkage.*

1. The check character (P) identifying the record type.
2. The unique number assigned to the particular patient.
3. Descriptive information about the patient.
4. Data for drugs 1, 2, ..., n used.
   a. Drug home address (Figure 58).
   b. Home address of another patient using the drug (Figure 59).
   c. Dosage information
5. Home address of the doctor treating the patient (Figure 60).
6. Special facility required by the patient 1, 2, ..., n.
   a. Facility home address (Figure 61).
   b. Home address of another patient using the same facility (Figure 62).
7. Data overflow address.
8. Category linkage (Figure 63).
9. Synonym linkage.

The doctor record identifies the particular doctor and to relate that record

The Structured Information File in Hospital Administration   93

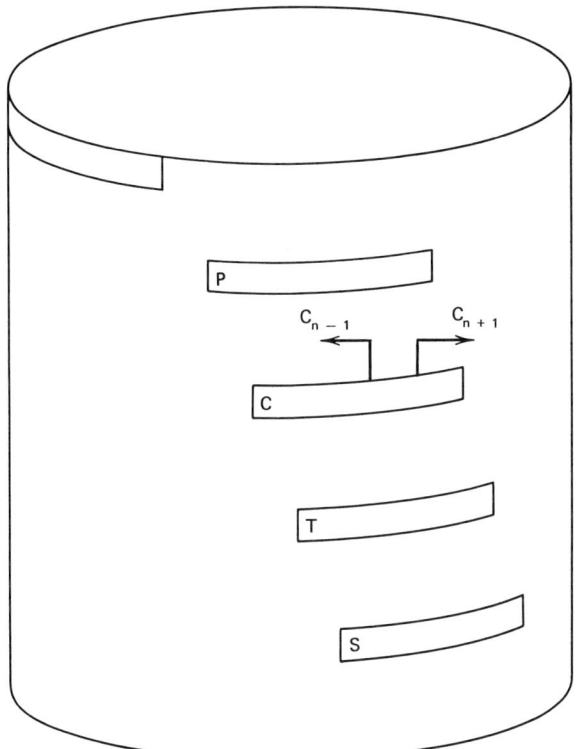

Figure 50.   *Course to course category linkage.*

to other pertinent records. The doctor's record might include the following.

1. The check character (M) identifying the particular type of record.
2. The unique number assigned to the doctor.
3. Descriptive information about the doctor.
4. Patient served data 1, 2, ..., n.
    a. Home address of the patient (Figure 64).
    b. Home address of another doctor treating the same patient (Figure 65).
5. Home address of a doctor to be consulted if this doctor is unavailable (Figure 66).
6. Data overflow address.
7. Category linkage (Figure 67).
8. Synonym linkage.

The drug record fully identifies the drug and relates it to the stream of data in the other records. Items contained within this record might be the following:

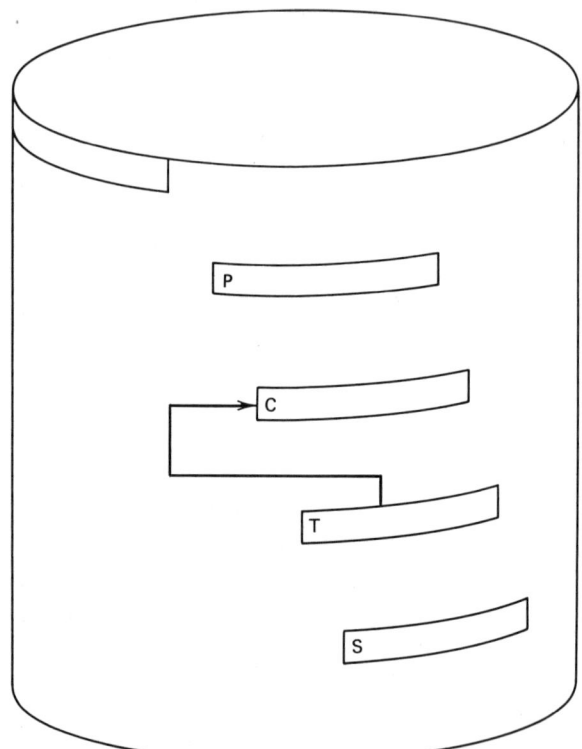

Figure 51.   *Teacher to course taught linkage.*

1. The check character (D) identifying the particular record type.
2. The unique number assigned to the drug.
3. Descriptive data about the drug.
4. The home address of one patient using the drug. (Figure 68).
5. Data overflow address.
6. Category linkage (Figure 69).
7. Synonym linkage.

The facility record defines a unique facility within the hospital such as a patient room, treatment room, operating room, etc., and relates the facility to the stream of data in the other records. A facility record might contain the following:

1. The check character (F) identifying the record type.
2. The identification number uniquely describing the facility.
3. The home address of a patient served by this facility (Figure 70).
4. The home address of a substitute facility. (Figure 71).
5. Data overflow address.

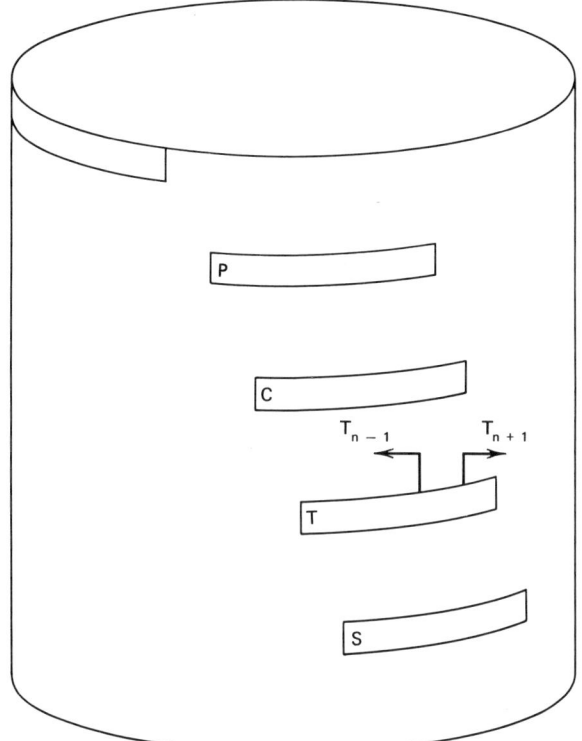

Figure 52. Teacher to teacher category linkage.

6. Category linkage (Figure 72).
7. Synonym linkage.

A hospital administration using a structured file system could retrieve necessary data on-line to answer specific operational control questions. For example, an immediate status of bed space might be obtained. Should a doctor be suddenly unable to attend his patients, the affected people could be readily identified and a referral doctor summoned. If a particular drug shipment failed to arrive, the patients involved could be identified and their doctors interrogated for substitute treatment. Each of the examples requires the information in at least two record types. The relationships are established in the structured information file concept, making available data not easily reached by conventional tape processing procedures. The complete structured information file for hospitals is conceptually displayed in Figure 73.

The usefulness of the structured information file for hospital administration can be described through the two applications previously mentioned.

A doctor with a number of patients in a hospital becomes ill himself.

96   Additional Structured Information File Applications

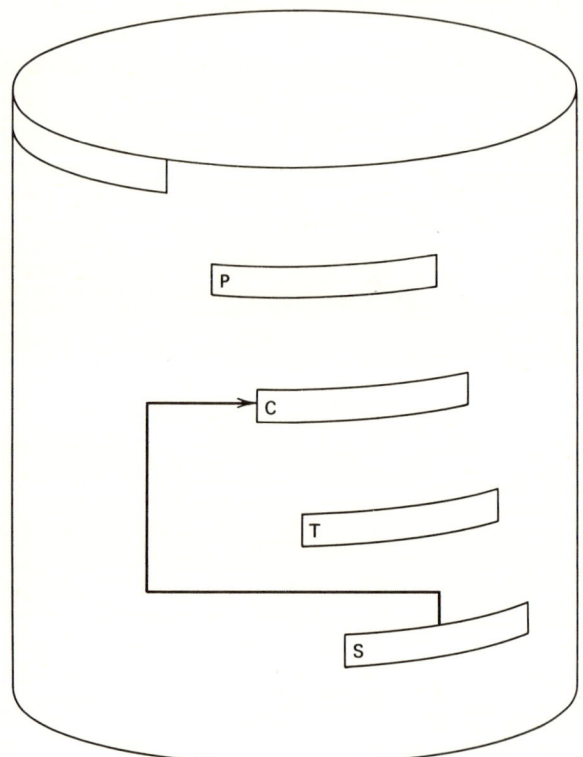

Figure 53.   School to course offered linkage.

Suddenly one of his patients requires particular attention. The patient record is accessed by randomizing, which references the assigned doctor. The doctor records will refer attention to alternate physicians to be consulted if the primary man is unavailable. These steps are shown in Figure 74.

Note that the structured file accommodates the contingency of the second doctor also being unavailable by finding a substitute. This is shown as a fourth step in Figure 75.

This particular example indicates potential design and program logic errors. Assume that the third doctor was also unavailable. Thus, as step 5, the record of his substitute is accessed. This is shown in Figure 76. Note the error! By referring back to doctor number one the three doctors have formed a closed loop. Unless contingencies such as these are foreseen, operational problems could arise.

A second application of the structured information file in hospital administration could involve drugs. Assume that the Food and Drug Administration discovers that a certain drug is defective and all use must cease. The hospital must identify all patients using the drug and contact each user's doctor for instructions. First, the drug is accessed by randomizing techniques. Second, the

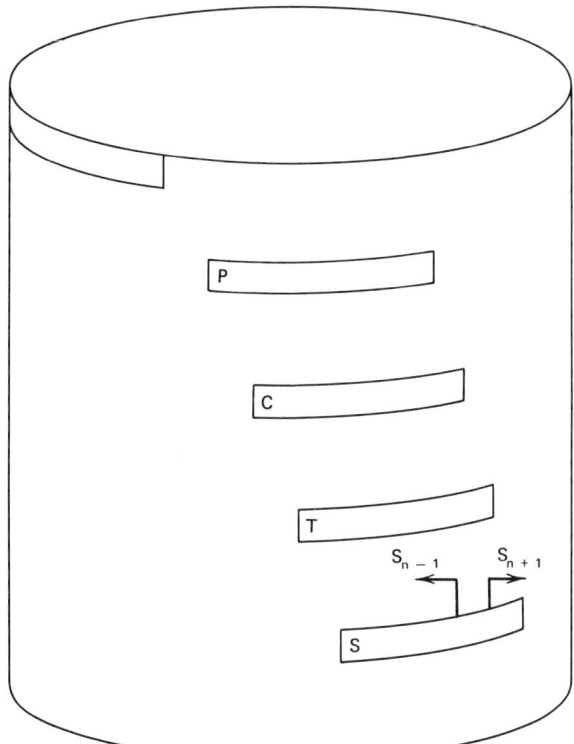

Figure 54. *School to school category linkage.*

drug record directs attention to a patient using the drug. Third, the patient record in turn directs attention to the patient's doctor. Fourth, the patient record provides a link to another patient using the same drug. This procedure is shown in Figure 77. Note that although the closed loop again occurs this time it is not only expected but anticipated.

C. AN IMPLICATION FOR PROCESSING LARGE TAPE FILES

While the structured information file described in the study has significant value as a management tool, converting to a random access data system would be a lengthy process. The immediate gain in the operating efficiency of a management information system would be the improvement of the slow processing of large-scale tape files.

An extrapolation of the analytical results of the structured file concept suggests the possibility of combining tape file processing with certain disk processing advantages.

98   *Additional Structured Information File Applications*

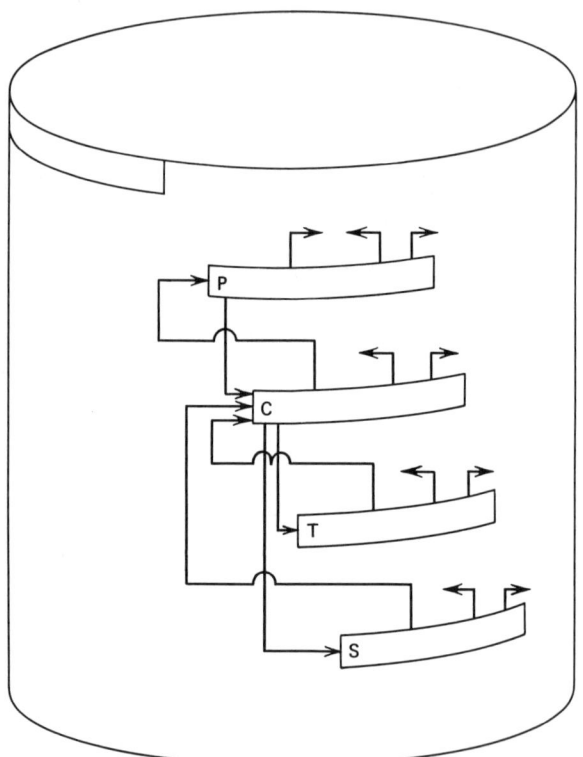

Figure 55.   *The steps to locate those pupils taught by a given teacher.*

The processing of large-scale files of information has long been a concern of the data processing community and both card and magnetic tape have been tried. The punched card concept was weak in many respects and attention was turned to the development of tape-oriented systems. Tape files permit the storage of large volumes of information in compact, easily stored containers. Processing of these files is sequential but can be accomplished at considerably higher speeds than is possible with card files. Tape files, however, must be stored off-line to the computing facility and must be physically placed on the tape handling units when desired. Thus in both the case of tapes and cards, the data are not immediately available. Storage of data on random access via disk eliminates the disadvantage of being off-line but does introduce an additional disadvantage. Random access memory devices are expensive, so the value of storing the information on-line must be weighed against the cost of having it there. It would appear that there must be some means of merging the two concepts to utilize the advantages of disk processing in handling large-scale tape files.

A methodology is suggested whereby specific random accessing techniques

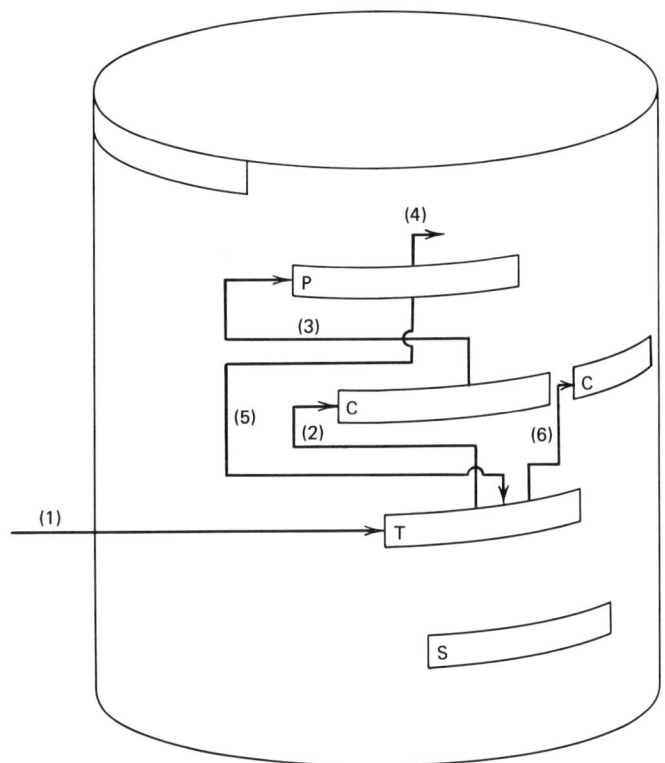

Figure 56. *Preparing report cards.*

are applied to the processing of tape information. For this discussion a set of assumptions are made relating to a large file processing operation. Assume there is a tape file containing five hundred reels which are in sequence, by an identification number. It is necessary to periodically process these tapes and update the information. It is further assumed that a disk storage device is available. The disk device need not be particularly large but it should be the size of a diskpack.

The suggested procedure is illustrated in Figure 78. A master identification tape, would be created that contains each of the identification numbers existing on the five hundred reel tape file. Figure 79 displays the process. The master identification file would then be loaded onto the disk and a series of transactions readied for processing. During some card-to-tape procedure, the particular characteristic number could be saved if the file were quite large. In any event, there would be some means of identification of each transaction that is required without actually having the full data set at this time.

Resident within memory, would be a five hundred bit indicator. Each bit of this indicator would be used to identify a given reel of tape. Each transaction,

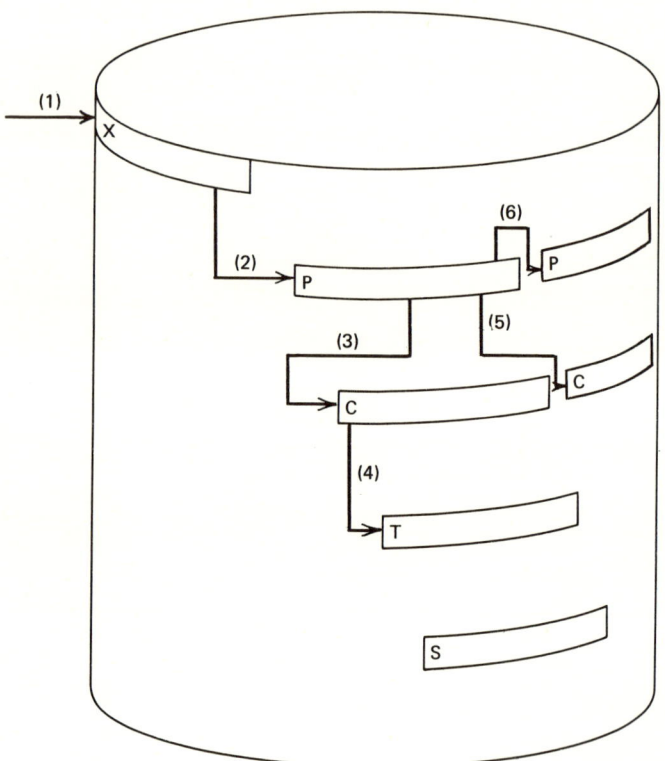

Figure 57. *The complete educational structured information file.*

identified by a characteristic identification number would be randomized to enter the disk file. This random process would examine the disk, identify the identification number, and, in this way, determine the record reel. The bit in the five hundred bit indicator representing the required tape reel would be activated. That activated bit corresponds to that reel to be sequentially passed. Once all the transaction identification numbers have been processed, the five hundred bit indicator will be partially turned on, i.e., some of the bit conditions on, others off. Thus only reels that need to be processed are those indicated by the bit indicators.

At this point, it would be possible with a small operating system for the console operator to scan the bit indicator and learn which is the first, second, third, etc., of these five hundred reels to be mounted. It would not necessarily be reel number one or reel number two, but the selection dictated by each successive bit showing in the on condition. These reels are mounted on the tape handling units and processed in a normal fashion. Each time a reel is completed the bit indicator is scanned for the next reel to be mounted. Thus, only those

An Implication for Processing Lage Tape Files 101

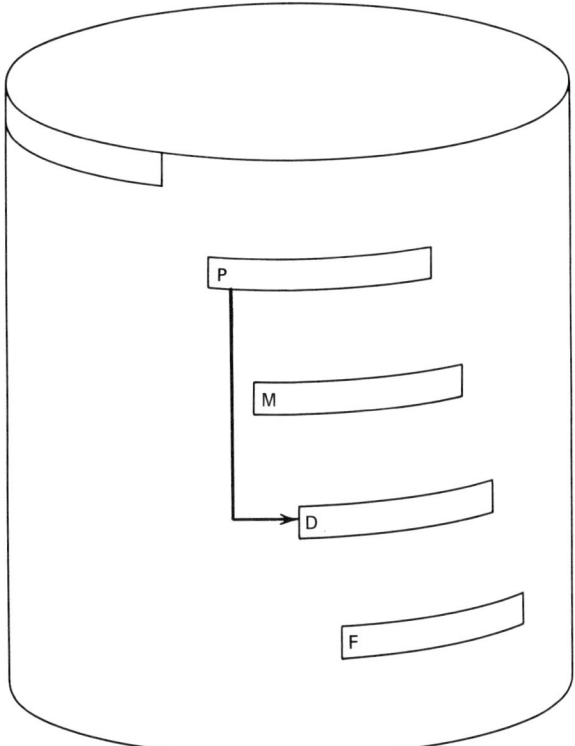

Figure 58. *Patient to drug used linkage.*

reels that need to be processed would physically be mounted on the tape units and processed through the computing system.

This suggested procedure for combining the advantages of tape and disk processing would alleviate the problems associated with the sequential processing of large-scale tape information files. The use of the disk and randomizing procedures identifies only those reels that should be processed. Again, the five hundred bit indicator gives notice as to which reels should be put on the units.

This method is probably of more value when the tape files are organized in a probabilistic manner rather than alphabetic or numeric. When the tape is in numeric sequence, there are simple means of identification. But the above procedure has merit. When the user departs from the conventional tape file organization and combines with randomizing for access, a whole new processing world opens.

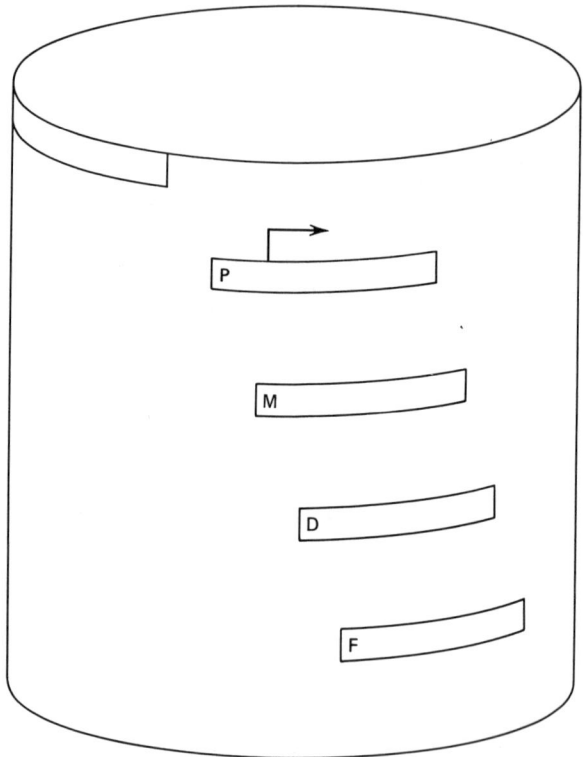

Figure 59. *Patient to another patient using same drug linkage.*

D. SUMMARY

This chapter described additional structured information file applications. The first considered the use in educational administration wherein the file completely integrates the records of pupils, teachers, courses, and schools. The second involved hospital administration with the records of patients, doctors, drugs, and facilities.

The third and final application presented an opportunity to improve the efficiency of processing large tape files. It utilizes a randomizing process to enter a random access file to determine on which tape the record is found.

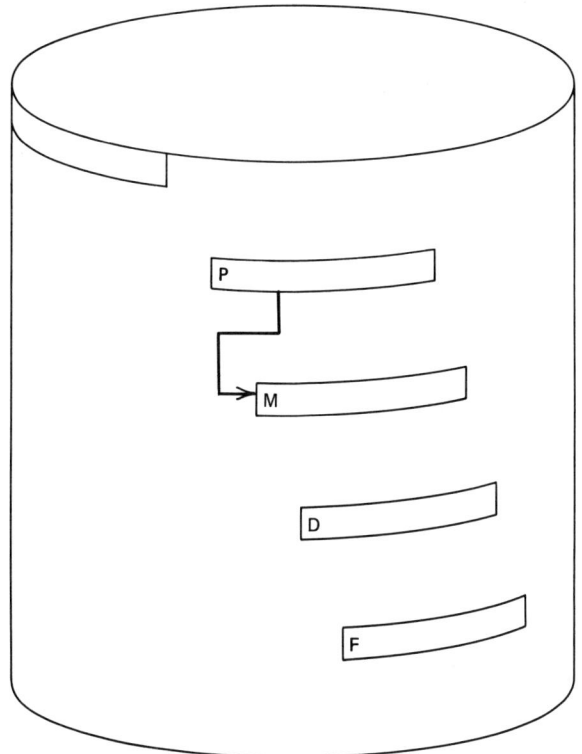

Figure 60. *Patient to attending doctor linkage.*

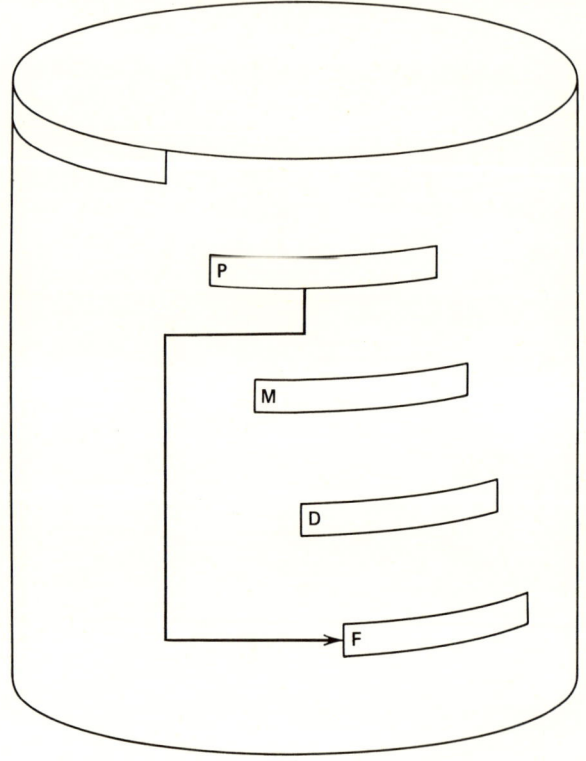

Figure 61. *Patient to facilities used linkage.*

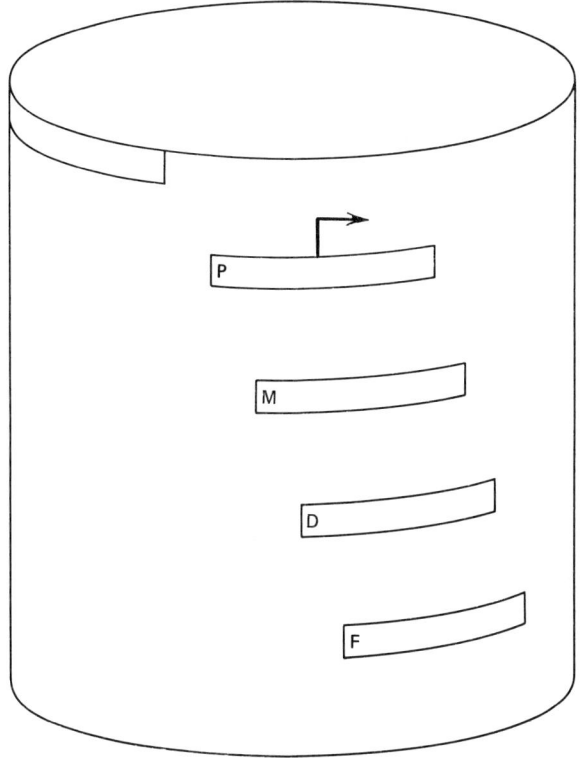

Figure 62. *Patient to another patient using same facility linkage.*

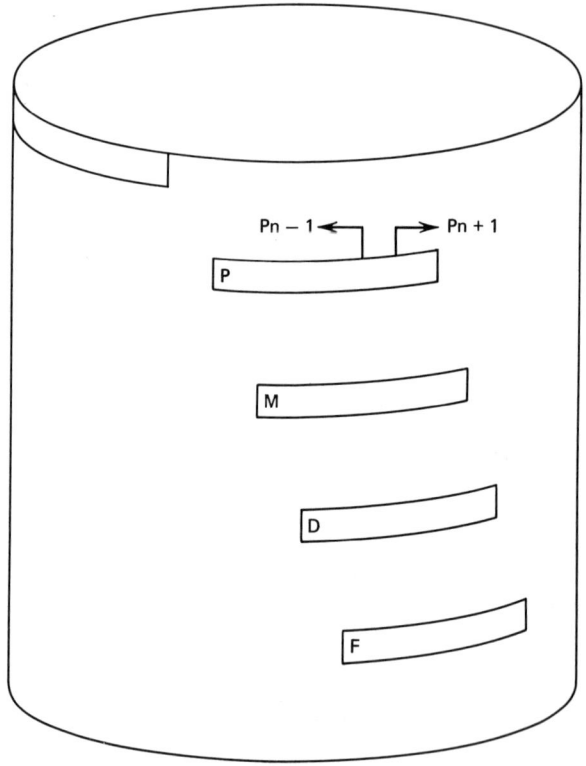

Figure 63. *Patient to patient category linkage.*

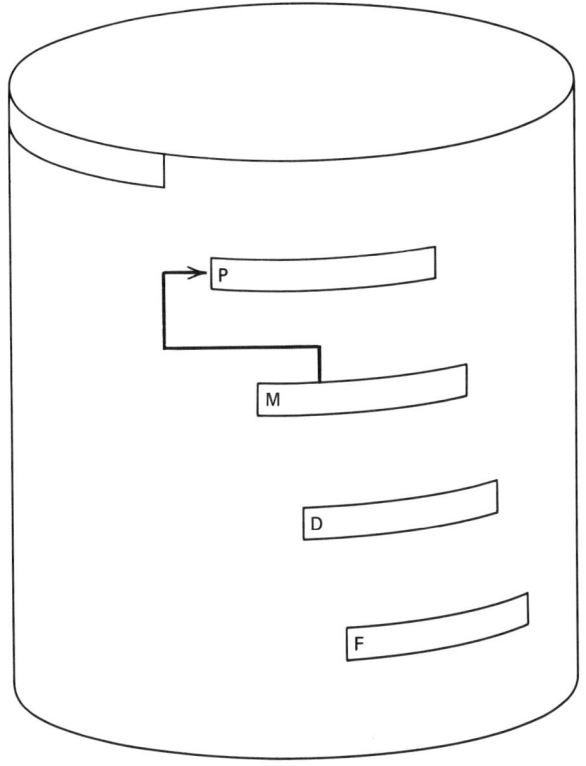

Figure 64. *Doctor to patient served linkage.*

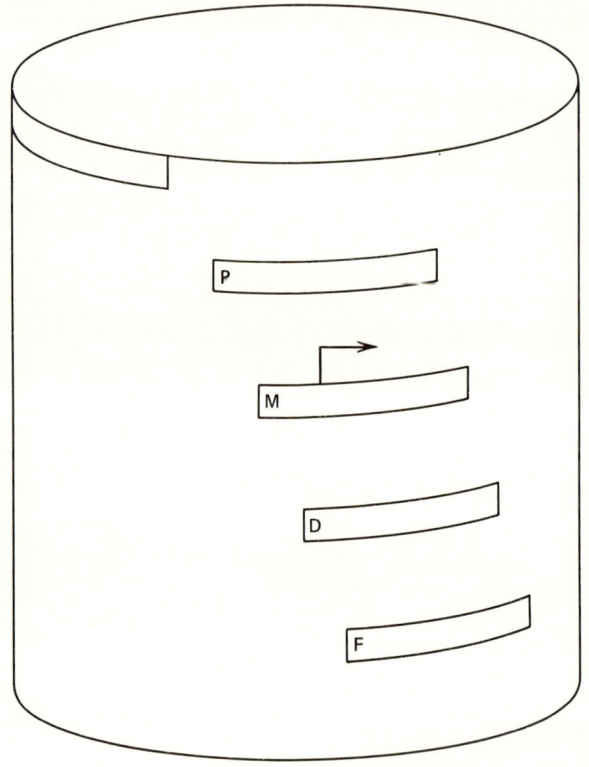

Figure 65. *Doctor to another doctor treating same patient linkage.*

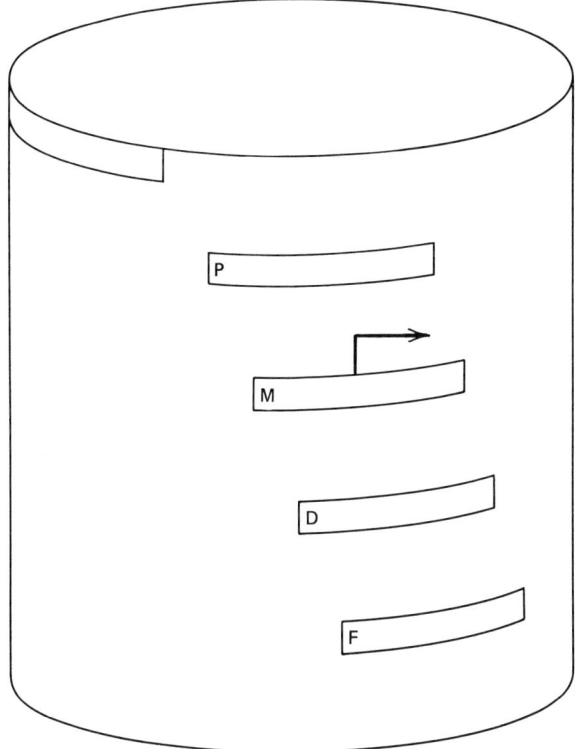

Figure 66. *Doctor to be consulted if primary doctor not available linkage.*

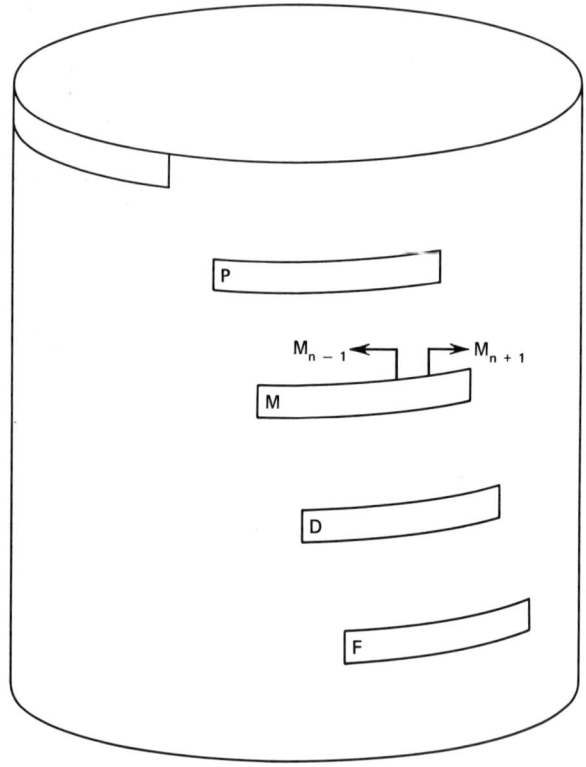

Figure 67. *Doctor to doctor category linkage.*

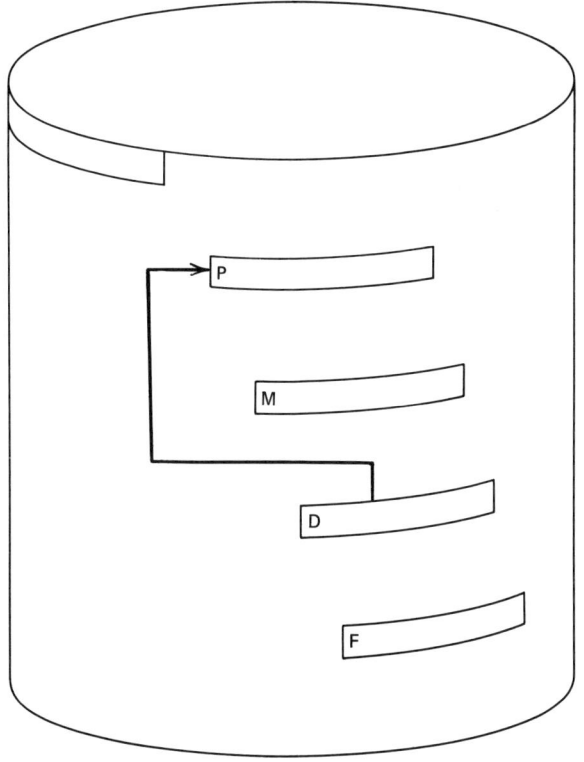

Figure 68. *Drug to using patient linkage.*

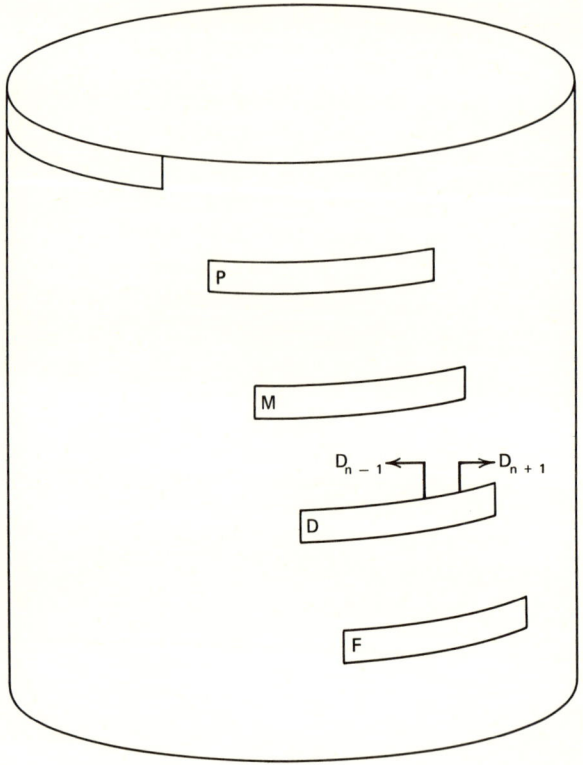

Figure 69.   *Drug to drug category linkage.*

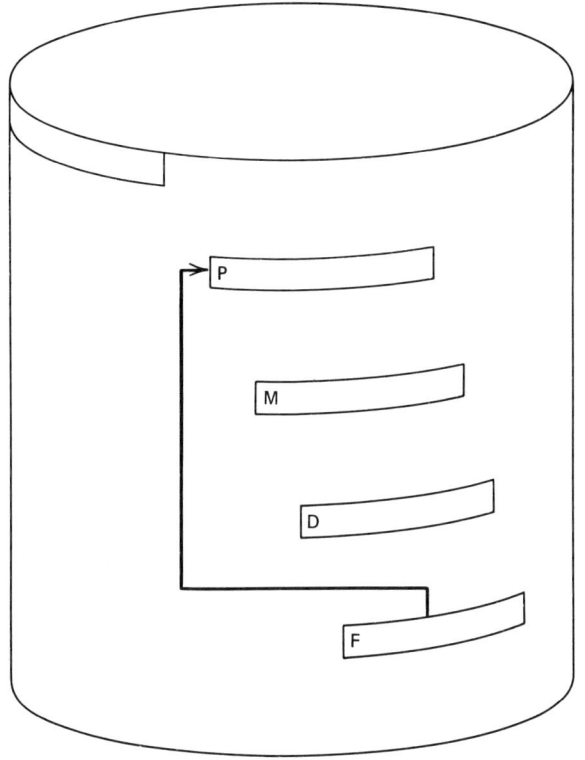

Figure 70. *Facility to using patient linkage.*

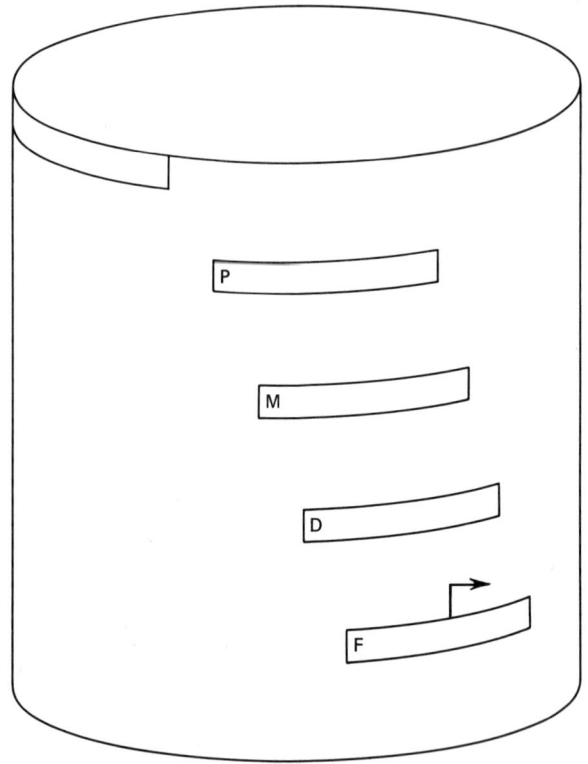

Figure 71. *Facility to substitute facility linkage.*

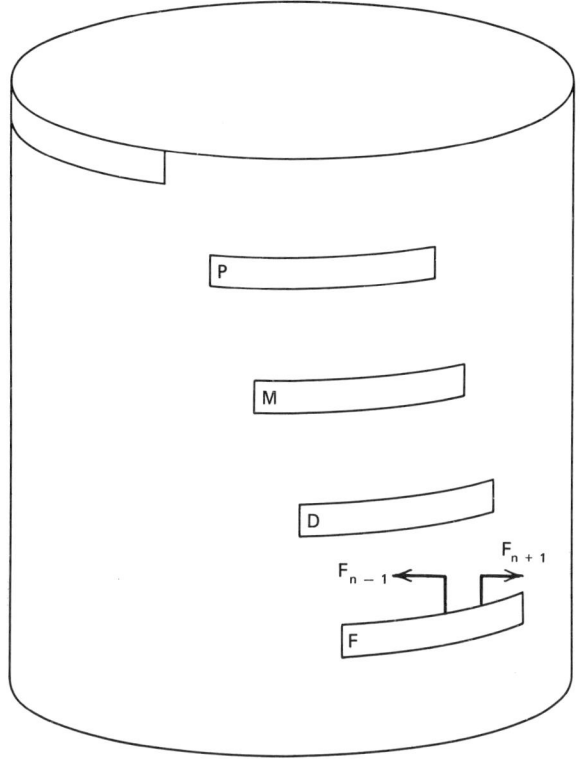

Figure 72. *Facility to facility category linkage.*

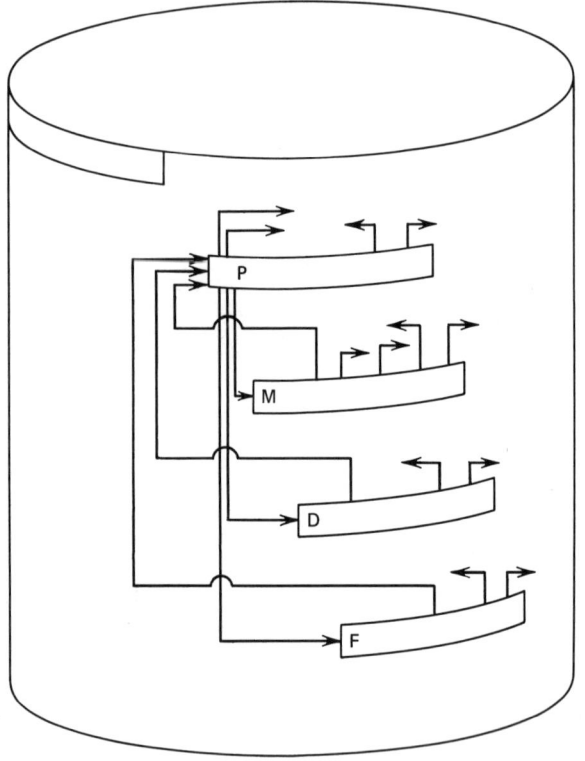

Figure 73. *The complete hospital structured information file.*

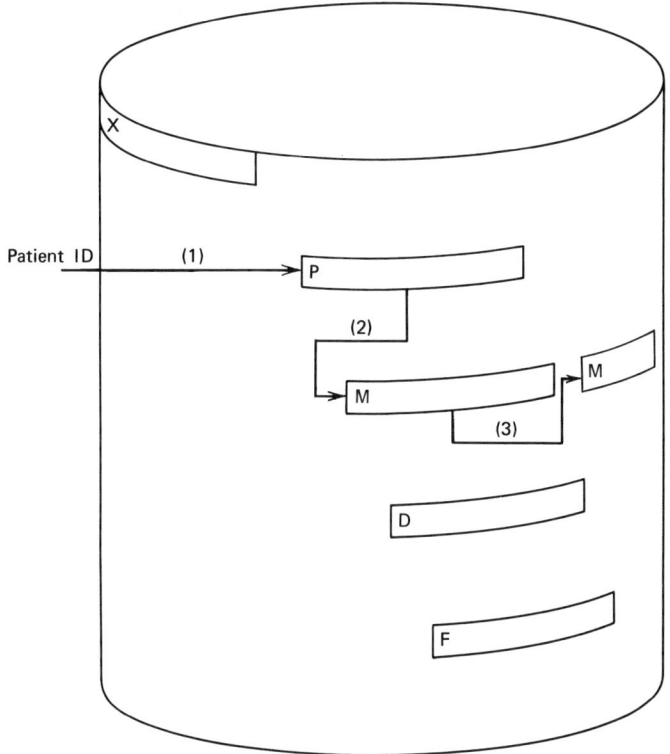

Figure 74. *Locating a substitute doctor.*

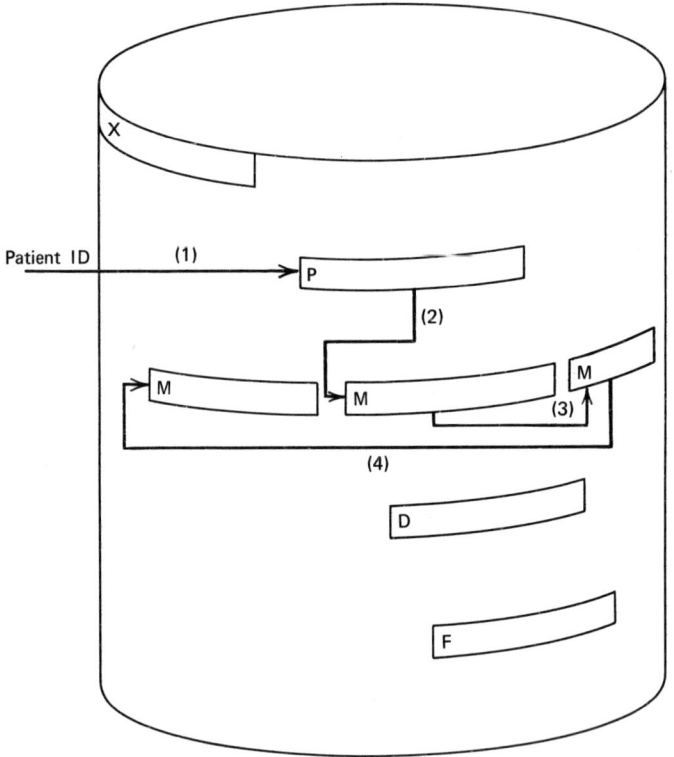

Figure 75. *Locating a substitute for a substitute doctor.*

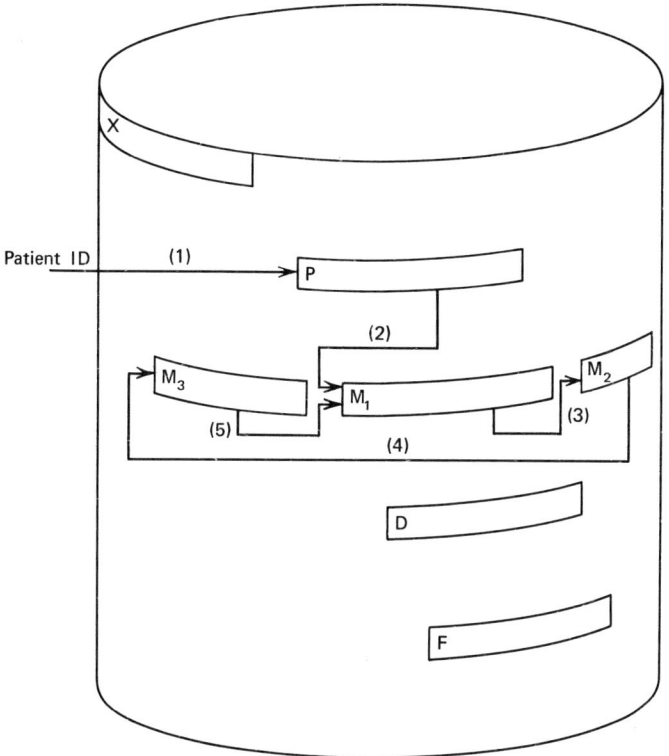

Figure 76. *The error of closed loop linkage.*

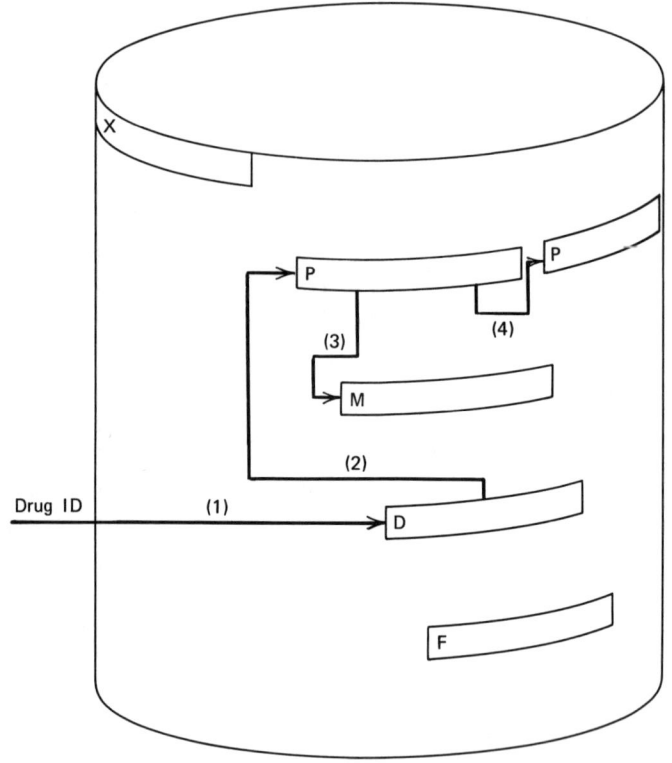

Figure 77. *Locating all patients using one drug and their doctors.*

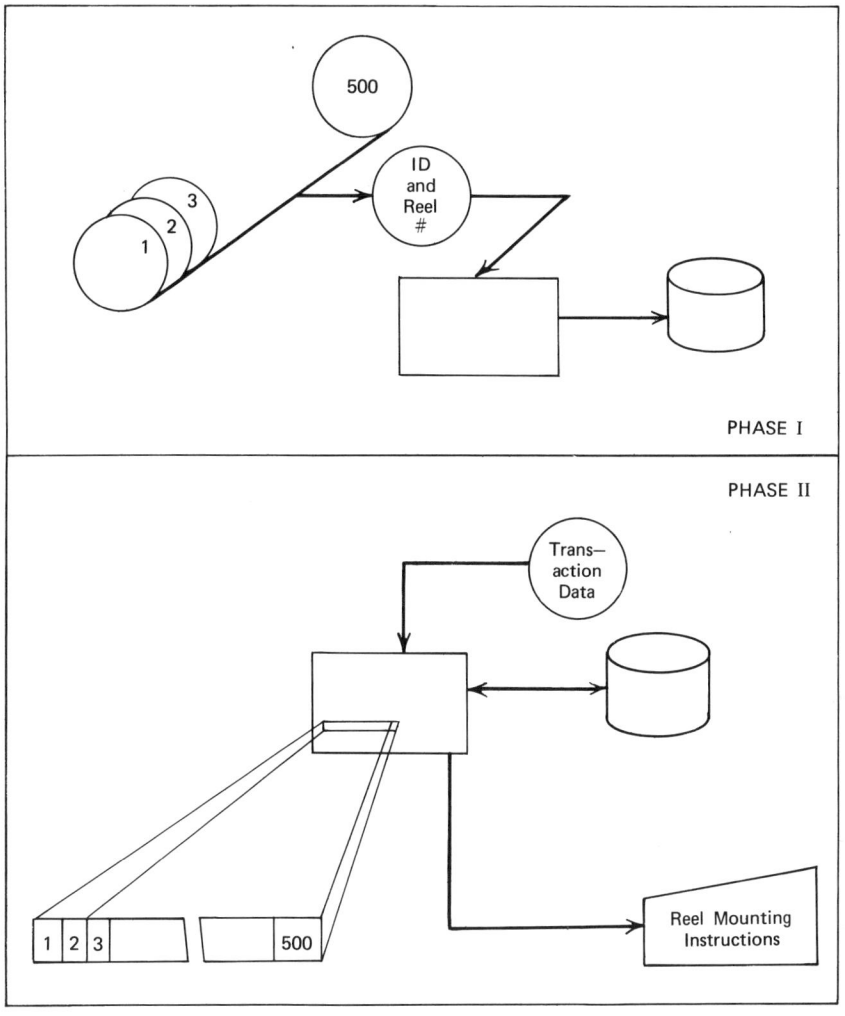

Figure 78. *Processing large tape files.*

Data ID Number	Reel Number	Disk Location	

Figure 79. *Master identification tape record.*

Seven

Summary

The material in this text has attempted to demonstrate and validate the nature and character of one approach to a structured information file. This requirement is a direct result of the growth of the economy, the subsequent enlargement of organizations since World War II, and the information explosion. Timely information has become an increasingly costly commodity indeed. Organizations attempting to cope with the growing information explosion, decentralized operations to maintain a close touch. The initial systems, designed to check the growing disparity in the timeliness of data were evidenced first in organizational change. However, once management realized the situation was beyond human capacities, attention was directed to electronic data processing.

While data processing was generically suited to solving routine management tasks, the basic philosophy was insensitive to the differences in specific information required by management to monitor the full range of corporate activities. Many attempts were made to integrate the entire battery of information processing tasks into a single, elaborate, computer-based total information system. Unwittingly the total system concept failed to recognize that there are dimensions and features of data requirements that cannot be subordinated to the view of a total information system. The timeliness and the specificity of data needs form the basis for discriminating between the various choices. Managerial functions would involve either strategic planning, managerial control, or operational control.

Each of these functions requires information with differing degrees of detail and response time and a unique approach must be taken for the data processing activities serving each particular level. The purpose of this work is the development of various operational control situations data management schemes.

Traditionally information has been mechanically processed either sequentially or randomly. Sequential processing requires the examination of every record preceding the desired record and is limited in speed of response. Random processing conquers that fault but requires complex and relatively expensive random access memory devices. But where a need exists, as in operational control situations, the expense is rewarded by timely information. One aspect of the material presented in this book was analytical, i.e., the derivation of a procedure for random entry to the structured information file. The second was descriptive, i.e., the design and validation of internal file linkages.

Three of the ten trial randomizing procedures yielded results and provide direction in the analysis of in-house data. The three procedures were: (1) squaring the characteristic number and selecting the middle five digits as the home address resulted in an average of 1.980, (2) selecting the five digit remainder after dividing by the largest prime number under the record capacity of the memory device produced an average of 1.380, and (3) extracting the two low order digits of sub-field one and the three low order digits of sub-field two and combining the numbers as the home address produced an average of 1.377.

In the design of the structured file itself, five elements were isolated that were considered common to each record class. They were:

1. A check character identifying the class of record.
2. An identification number identifying the particular record of the class.
3. A data overflow linkage to point to a home address containing additional data about each record.
4. A category linkage that logically relates each record to another record of the same class, thus creating a chain of all records of this class.
5. A synonym linkage that points to another home address to examine to find a nominated record. The synonym linkages create a chain of records whose identification numbers all randomized to the same home address.

In addition to these five common elements, each record class has specific linkages in a unique format to complete the logical relationships for the structured file concept. The linkages are designed to permit actual data to be recorded in only one location in the system. For example, products that were stored in any warehouse, sold by any salesmen, and produced at any facility were identified by the same three-digit home address in each appropriate record. Detailed information about the product such as the 20-character description and the seven-character cost items were stored in the product record only.

Sub-chains of data items within a class were also developed and maintained where appropriate. For instance, the format of the salesman's record included a field for each product sold. A sub-field within each of those fields was a linkage to another salesman's record who sold the same product. In full scale use, these sub-chains would substantially reduce processing time although they were not particularly required for a small scale model.

To illustrate the validity of the model, a program was written to prepare typical business reports—a sales report for each salesman, a quantity on-hand report for each product, and a report of the needs of each warehouse and the capacities of each production facility in conjunction with the cost of transportation between each warehouse-facility pair for each product. Since each record required data from different record classes and was required to extract those data in a random fashion, the successful preparation of the reports supported the claim that the model does function as intended.

To further view the usefulness of the design concept, the discussion identified the potential for application of structured files in hospital and educational administration. The hospital example related doctors, patients, drugs, and facilities while the educational example related pupils, teachers, courses, and schools. Records for each class of data in both examples contained the same five common elements and specific data and linkages appropriate to each.

The structured information file concept offers a data management philosophy for use in operational control environments. Since data at this level of management activity must be both specific and timely, a unique information processing capability is needed. Structured files, as described in this study, offer this potential.

Eight

Suggested Problems

The problems listed in this chapter cover a wide scope and range from the simple, short-answer variety to the more complex. The more time-consuming problems should be considered as major tasks.

In the latter instances the student is required to gather data sets, perform the systems design activity, write the programs, develop test data, debug the system, debug the programs, and run the large data set.

1. Compare and contrast card versus tape processing.
2. Compare and contrast tape versus disk processing for a given task on cost or economic bases.
3. Compare and contrast tape versus disk processing for a given task on a time basis.
4. Compare and contrast tape versus disk processing for a given task on the basis of file size.
5. Compare and contrast tape versus disk processing for a given task on a read-write speed basis.
6. Compare and contrast tape versus disk processing for a given task on the basis of logical comparison speeds.
7. Compare and contrast tape versus disk processing for a given task on the basis of cycle times.
8. How do you characterize stored information?
9. The structured information file concept is predicated on the rule that a piece of data should be stored in one place and only one place. The alternative is to store that piece of data in each place that it is required. Compare these two views for
    a. Tape processing.
    b. Disk processing.

Suggested Problems 127

10. Compare the multiply recorded data concept on tape versus the singly stored data concept on disk for multi-level files.
11. How is a tape file updated?
12. How is a disk file updated?
13. What are the inherent dangers of recording updated information in the same place as the old data on a disk record?
14. How do you guarantee that the data in the file are 100% accurate?
15. Design a system to assure management that the file will never be accidentally destroyed?
16. What are the current applications of the structured information file concept?
17. What are the future applications for the structured information file concept?
18. Describe the difference between random and sequential file organization.
19. Describe the difference between random and sequential file processing.
20. Describe how you might sequentially process a file organized randomly on
    a. card
    b. tape
    c. disk
21. Describe how you might randomly process a file organized sequentially on
    a. card
    b. tape
    c. disk
22. What are the common elements of a random access file record?
23. Could the identification number of a record in a structured information file have an exact duplicate?
24. Does the concept of overflow apply to index sequential? If so, how would it be accomplished?
25. Do all record categories need linkages to every other category? Give examples to support your answer.
26. Compare the Library Science view of Information Retrieval with the view expressed in this book.
27. How can efficient record placement be accomplished in the structured information file concept?
28. Discuss the factors of inefficiency resulting from continual processing of data on random access files.
29. Design a system to cope with the above problem.
30. What effect does the packing density have on the randomizing algorithm?

31. What effect does the packing density have on the index sequential method?

32. What effect does the packing density have on the indexing method?

33. Compare and contrast the control record in the structured file concept with the cylinder and surface index in the index sequential approach.

34. Compare and contrast index sequential versus structured files for sequential tasks.

35. Compare and contrast index sequential versus structured files for non-sequential processing tasks.

36. Prepare a logic flowchart for adding or deleting a record to your structured information file.

37. Describe how the salesman file should be linked to permit processing in social security number order.

38. Compare the index sequential methodology with the processing of large tape files using the concept of the randomizing access methods.

39. Assume that a list of school athletes are to be excused from classes for a two-day trip. Prepare a list to be given to each teacher containing the names of all athletes in the teacher's classes.

40. Describe how you would prepare a schedule for using the specific facilities of a hospital.

41. Gather a large set of numbers as ID for a file, i.e., 10,000.

42. Write the programs to evaluate some of the suggested approaches for randomizing.

43. Devise an algorithm of your own. Evaluate it.

44. Gather a small set of data revolving about at least four categories of information.

45. Design a structured information file.

46. Write programs to create it.

47. Design a set of reports that require data from more than one category.

48. Write the programs to maintain the file, i.e., to add and delete records as well as to update data fields.

Bibliography

A. BOOKS

Awad, E. Business Data Processing. New York: Prentice-Hall, Inc., 1965.

Baum, C. and L. Gorsuch. Proceedings of the Second Symposium on Computer-Centered Data Base Systems. Santa Monica, Calif.: Systems Development Corp., 1965.

Becker, J. and R. Hayes. Information Storage and Retrieval: Tools, Elements, Theories. New York: John Wiley and Sons, 1963.

Berkeley, E. The Computer Revolution. Garden City, New York: Doubleday and Co., 1962.

Davis, G. An Introduction to Electronic Computers. New York: McGraw-Hill Book Co., 1965.

Davis, G. An Introduction to the IBM/360 Computer. New York: McGraw-Hill Book Co., 1965.

Davis, G. Computer Data Processing. New York: McGraw-Hill Book Co., 1973, p. 356.

Desmonde, W. Computers and Their Uses. Englewood Cliffs, N.J.: Prentice-Hall, Inc., 1964.

Eckman, D. Systems: Research and Design. New York: John Wiley and Sons, Inc., 1961.

Fairthorne, R. Towards Information Retrieval. London: Butterworthy, 1961.

Fisher, P. and G. Swindle. Computer Programming Systems. New York: Holt, Rinehart and Winston, 1964.

Flanagan, J. The Project Talent Data Bank. Pittsburgh, Pa.: University of Pittsburgh, 1965.

Greenberger, M. Computers and the World of the Future. Cambridge, Mass.: MIT Press, 1962.

Gregory, R. and R. Van Horn. Automatic Data Processing Systems. Belmont, Calif.: Wadsworth Publishing Co., 1964.

Hattey, L. and E. McCormick (eds.). Information Retrieval Management. Detroit: American Data Processing, Inc., 1962.

Howerton, P. Information Handling: First Principles. Washington, D.C.: Spartan Books, 1963.

Bibliography

Ideas for Management. Cleveland: Systems and Procedures Assoc., 1966.

Johnson, R. et al. The Theory and Management of Systems. New York: McGraw-Hill Book Co., 1963.

Kent, A. and O. Taulbee. Electronic Information Handling. Washington, D.C.: Spartan Books, 1965.

Kent, A. Textbook on Mechanized Information Retrieval. New York: Interscience Publishers, 1966.

McCracken, D. A Guide to COBOL Programming. New York: John Wiley and Sons, 1963.

McDonaugh, G. and J. Garrett. Management Systems, Working Concepts and Practices. Homewood, Ill.: Richard Irwin Co., 1965.

Meacham, A. and V. Thompson (eds.). Total Systems. Detroit: American Data Processing, Inc., 1962.

Meredith, W. Basic Mathematical and Statistical Tables for Psychology and Education. New York: McGraw-Hill Book Co., 1967.

NEAT/3. Dayton: National Cash Register Co., 1968, pp. 5-13.

Newman, S. Information Systems Compatibility. New York: Spartan Books, 1965.

Oakford, R. An Introduction to Electronic Data Processing Equipment. New York: McGraw-Hill Book Co., 1962.

Optner, S. Systems Analysis. Englewood Cliffs, N.J.: Prentice-Hall, Inc., 1965.

Parkhill, D. F. The Challenge of the Computer Utility. Reading, Mass.: Addison-Wesley Publishing Co., 1966.

Perry, J. Documentation and Information Retrieval. Cleveland: Western Re-Serve University Press, 1957.

Price, W. Introduction to Data Processing. San Francisco: Rinehart Press, 1972, p. 226.

Prince, T. Information Systems for Management Planning and Control. Homewood, Ill.: Richard D. Irwin, 1966.

Putnam, A., et al. Unified Operations Management. New York: McGraw-Hill Book Co., 1963.

Raun, D. An Introduction to COBOL Programming for Accounting and Business Analyses. Belmont, Calif.: Dickenson Publishing Co., 1966.

Schmidt, R. and W. Meyers. Electronic Business Data Processing. New York: Holt, Rinehart, and Winston, 1963.

Sharp, H. Readings in Information Retrieval. New York: Scarecrow Press, 1964.

Sharp, J. Some Fundamentals of Information Retrieval. London: Andre Deutsch, Ltd., 1965.

Shultz, R. and T. Whisler. Management Organization and the Computer. Glencoe, Ill.: Free Press, Inc., 1960.

Simonton, W. Information Retrieval Today. Minneapolis: University of Minnesota, 1962.

Stevens, N. A Comparative Study of Three Systems of Information Retrieval. New Brunswick, N.J.: Rutgers University, 1961.

Taubes, M. and H. Wooster. Information Storage and Retrieval. New York: Columbia University Press, 1958.

Taunt, J. Digital Tape Drives. Elmhurst, Ill.: Business Press, 1965.

Tomeski, E., et al. (eds.). The Clarification, Unification, and Integration of Information, Storage and Retrieval. New York: Management Dynamics Corp., 1961.

Vickery, B. On Retrieval Systems Theory. Washington, D.C.: Butterworth, Inc., 1965.

Williams, W. Principles of Automated Information Retrieval. Elmhurst, Ill.: Business Press, 1965.

Withington, F. The Uses of Computers in Business Organizations. Reading, Mass.: Addison-Wesley, Inc., 1966.

B. PERIODICALS

Bachman, C. "Software for Random Access Processing," Datamation, April, 1965, pp. 32-38.

Blumberg, D. "Information Systems and the Planning Process," Data Processing Magazine, May, 1966, pp. 17-26.

Blumenthal, R. "Management in Real-Time," Data Processing Magazine, April, 1965, pp. 18-23.

Bucholz, W. "File Organization and Addressing," IBM Systems Journal, June, 1963, pp. 86-111.

Burlingame, J. "Information Technology and Decentralization," Harvard Business Review, November-December, 1961, pp. 121-126.

Cheydleur, B. "Information Retrieval, 1966," Datamation, October, 1961, pp. 21-25.

"Computer-Assisted Legal Research," Oregon Law Review, Summer, 1972, pp. 665-696.

Dearden, J. "Can Management Information Be Automated?" Harvard Business Review, November-December, 1962, pp. 128-135.

Dearden, J. "How to Organize Information Systems," Harvard Business Review, March-April, 1965, pp. 65-73.

Dearden, J. "MIS is a Mirage," Harvard Business Review, January-February, 1972, pp. 90-99.

Dearden, J. "Myth of Real-Time Management Information," Harvard Business Review, May-June, 1966, pp. 123-132.

Gurk, H. and J. Menker. "The Design and Simulation of an Information Processing System," ACM Journal, April, 1961, pp. 260-270.

Hartmann, J. "Management Control in Real-Time is the Objective," Systems and Procedures Journal, September, 1965, pp. 26-28.

Harvey, A. "Systems Can Too be Practical," Business Horizons, Summer, 1964, pp. 56-69.

Herner, S. "Methods of Organizing Information for Storage and Searching," American Documentation, January, 1962, pp. 3-14.

Hockman, J. "Specification for an Integrated Management Information System," Systems and Procedures Journal, January-February, 1963, pp. 40-41.

Kaimann, R. "Entry to the File: Randomize or Index," Data Processing, December, 1966, pp. 18-21.

Kaimann, R., et al. "Attendance Accounting: Yesterday, Today, and Tomorrow," Journal of Educational Data Processing, Summer, 1966, pp. 119-133.

Leavitt, H. and T. Whistler. "Management in the 1980's," Harvard Business Review, November-December, 1958, pp. 41-48.

Margaritis, P. "A Real-Time Management Information Retrieval System," Data Processing Magazine, July, 1965, pp. 21-26.

Martino, R. "The Development and Installation of a Total Management System," Data Processing for Management, April, 1963, pp. 31-37.

Martins, G. "Some Comments on Information Retrieval," Datamation, December, 1964, pp. 24-27.

Moravec, A. "Basic Concepts for Designing Fundamental Information Systems," Management Services, July-August, 1965, pp. 37-45.

Nicolaus, J. "The Automated Approach to Technical Information Retrieval," Naval Engineers Journal, October, 1964, pp. 715-27.

Oldehoeft, A. "The Roles of Systems Analysis, Programming, and Operations in an Information System," Educational Data Processing Newsletter, April, 1964, pp. 1-4.

Parker, J. "The Sabre System," Datamation, September, 1965, pp. 49-52.

Peterson, W. "Addressing for Random Access Storage," IBM Journal of Research and Development, April, 1957, pp. 130-146.

Ream, N. "On-Line Management Information," Datamation, March, 1964, pp. 27-30.

Schay, A. and N. Raver. "A Method for Key-to-Address Transformation," IBM Journal of Research and Development, April, 1963, pp. 121-126.

Shaw, R. "Information Retrieval," Science, July, 1964, pp. 606-609.

Spaulding, A. "Is the Total Systems Concept Practical?" Systems and Procedures Journal, January-February, 1964, pp. 28-32.

Stuart, S. "Crystal Balling: New Challenges for Chief Executives," Infosystems, January, 1973, p. 22.

Swets, J. "Information Retrieval Systems," Science, July, 1963, pp. 245-250.

Thurston, P. "Who Should Control Information Systems?" Harvard Business Review, November-December, 1962, pp. 135-139.

"Unified Operations Management," Business Automation, January, 1962, pp. 26-31.

Wilson, H. "A Hospital Patient Data System," Data Processing for Management, May, 1963, pp. 21-24.

C. ARTICLES IN COLLECTIONS

Atherton, P. "File Organization," in Howerton, P. Information Handling: First Principles, Washington, D.C., Spartan Books, Inc., 1961, pp. 19-54.

Bachman, C. "Integrated Data Store," in Baum, C. Proceedings of the Second Symposium on Computer-Centered Data Base Systems. Santa Monica, Calif.: Systems Development Corp., 1965, pp. 3.231-3.275.

Beatty, J. and S. Muroga. "File Memory Addressing," in Kochen, M. Some Problems in Information Science. New York: Scarecrow Press, pp. 206-216.

Castleman, P. A. "On-Line Data Management for the Massachusetts General Hospital," in Baum, C. Proceedings of the Second Symposium on Computer-Centered Data Base Systems. Santa Monica, Calif.: Systems Development Corp., 1965, pp. 3.143-3.184.

Costello, J. "Indexing in Depth: Practical Parameters," in Howerton, P. Information Handling: First Principles. Washington, D.C.: Spartan Books, 1963, pp. 55-58.

Garland, J. "Optimizing Information Searches," in Howerton, P. Information Handling: First Principles. Washington, D.C.: Spartan Books, 1963, pp. 89-106.

Kaimann, R. "Project TUHL: An Integrated Educational Data Bank," in Goodman, E. Automated Education Handbook. Detroit: Automated Education Center, pp. IV A 23-31.

Luhn, H. "Automated Intelligence Systems—Some Basic Problems and Requisites for Their Solution," in Tomeski, E. The Clarification, Unification, and Integration of Information, Storage, and Retrieval. New York: Management Dynamics Corp., 1961, pp. 3-22.

Opler, A. "Information Retrieval by Digital Computer—Reality or Myth," Tomeski, E. et al. The Clarification, Unification, and Integration of Information, Storage, and Retrieval. New York: Management Dynamics Corp., 1961, pp. 69-78.

Reich, D. "Associative Memories and Information Retrieval," in Kochen, M. Some Problems in Information Science. New York: Scarecrow Press, 1965, pp. 211-235.

Salzer, J. "Evolutionary Design of Complex Systems," in Eckman, D. Systems: Research and Design. New York: John Wiley and Sons, Inc., 1961, pp. 197-215.

D. PUBLICATIONS OF THE GOVERNMENT AND OTHER ORGANIZATIONS

International Business Machines Corporation. Disk Storage Concepts. White Plains, N.Y.: International Business Machines Corp., 1963.

Bibliography

_____. Generalized Information System. White Plains, N.Y.: International Business Machines Corp., 1971, p. 1.

_____. Generalized Information System/2. White Plains, N.Y.: International Business Machines Corp., 1971, p. 1.

_____. IBM 2311 Disk Storage Drive. White Plains, N.Y.: International Business Machines Corp., 1966.

_____. IBM 2841 Storage Control Unit. White Plains, N.Y.: International Business Machines Corp., 1966.

_____. IBM System/360 Disk and Tape Operating Systems COBOL Language Specifications. White Plains, N.Y.: International Business Machines Corp., 1966.

_____. IBM System/360 Disk and Tape Operating Systems COBOL Programmers Guide. White Plains, N.Y.: International Business Machines Corp., 1966.

_____. IBM System/360 Disk Operating Systems Data Management Concepts. White Plains, N.Y.: International Business Machines Corp., 1966.

_____. IBM System/360 Disk and Tape Operating System Utility Programs Specifications. White Plains, N.Y.: International Business Machines Corp., 1966.

_____. Reference Manual 1401 Data Processing System. White Plains, N.Y.: International Business Machines Corp., 1961.

U.S. Senate, Committee on Government Operations. Coordination of Information on Federal Research and Development Projects in the Field of Electronics. Washington, D.C.: Government Printing Office, 1961.

University Computer Center. UCC DOS User's Guide. Iowa City: University Computer Center, 1966.

Appendix

The Ten Trial Randomizers and Their Results

The appendix contains the results of the ten trial randomizers. Each randomizing algorithm is repeated here and the results of that algorithm are tabulated.

TRIAL NUMBER 1

This trial takes the remainder after division by 100,000.
    I.D. Number   123456789
    Home Address   56789

TABLE 39. Trial 1 Results

Synonyms	Frequency	Percent	Cumulative Percent
0	6480.	13.2380	13.2380
1	1004.	4.1021	17.3401
2	537.	3.2911	20.6313
3	248.	2.0266	22.6578
4	291.	1.9510	24.6088
5	144.	1.7651	26.3739
6	137.	1.9591	28.3330
7	110.	1.7978	30.1307
8	85.	1.5628	31.6936

TABLE 39. Trial 1 Results (continued)

Synonyms	Frequency	Percent	Cumulative Percent
9	69.	1.4096	33.1032
10	60.	1.3483	34.4515
11	47.	1.1522	35.6037
12	32.	0.8498	36.4535
13	24.	0.6864	37.1399
14	40.	1.2257	38.3657
15	20.	0.6537	39.0194
16	17.	0.5904	39.6098
17	18.	0.6619	40.2717
18	19.	0.7375	41.0092
19	31.	1.2666	42.2758
20	35.	1.5015	43.7773
21	23.	1.0337	44.8110
22	30.	1.4086	46.2206
23	23.	1.1277	47.3483
24	17.	0.8682	48.2165
25	20.	1.0623	49.2789
26	19.	1.0480	50.3269
27	18.	1.0296	51.3565
28	15.	0.8887	52.2451
29	18.	1.1032	53.3483
30	13.	0.8233	54.1716
31	14.	0.9152	55.0868
32	14.	0.9438	56.0306
33	7.	0.4862	56.5168
34	18.	1.2870	57.8039
35	11.	0.9561	58.7600
36	11.	0.9070	59.6670
37	16.	1.2421	60.9091
38	13.	0.0358	61.9448
39	10.	0.8172	62.7620
40	14.	1.1726	63.9346
41	18.	1.5444	65.4791
42	19.	1.6691	67.1481
43	13.	1.1685	68.3166
44	15.	1.3790	69.6956
45	19.	1.7855	71.4811
46	9.	0.8641	72.3452
47	19.	1.8631	74.2084
48	10.	1.0010	75.2094
49	16.	1.6343	76.8437
50	15.	1.5628	78.4065
51	8.	0.8498	79.2564
52	10.	1.0827	80.3391
53	6.	0.6619	81.0010
54	13.	1.4607	82.4617
55	9.	1.0296	83.4913

TABLE 39. Trial 1 Results (continued)

Synonyms	Frequency	Percent	Cumulative Percent
56	10.	1.1645	84.6558
57	6.	0.7109	85.3667
58	10.	1.2053	86.5720
59	7.	0.8580	87.4300
60	2.	0.2492	87.6792
61	9.	1.1399	88.8192
62	5.	0.6435	89.4627
63	6.	0.7845	90.2472
64	5.	0.6639	90.9111
65	9.	1.2135	92.1246
66	4.	0.5475	92.6721
67	6.	0.8335	93.5056
68	6.	0.8458	94.3514
69	7.	1.0010	95.3524
70	5.	0.7552	96.0776
71	4.	0.5884	96.6660
72	2.	0.2983	96.9642
73	5.	0.7559	97.7201
74	1.	0.1532	97.8733
75	2.	0.3105	98.1838
76	0.	0.0000	98.1838
77	2.	0.3187	98.5025
78	2.	0.3228	98.8253
79	0.	0.0000	98.8253
80	3.	0.4964	99.3217
81	2.	0.3350	99.6568
82	1.	0.1696	99.8263
83	0.	0.0000	99.8263
84	1.	0.1736	100.0000

Total number of input records	48950
Total number of home addresses generated	9996
Total number of accesses	751844
Average number of accesses	15.359

TRIAL NUMBER 2

This trial selects the middle five digits from the square of the characteristic number.

I.D. Number	123456789
(I.D. No.)^2	15241578750190521
Home Address	78750

TABLE 40. Trial 2 Results

Synonyms	Frequency	Percent	Cumulative Percent
0	16649.	34.0123	34.0123
1	4490.	18.3453	52.3575
2	2219.	13.5996	65.9571
3	1405.	11.4811	77.4382
4	985.	9.0398	86.4780
5	520.	6.3739	92.8519
6	277.	3.9612	96.8131
7	114.	1.8631	98.6762
8	50.	0.9193	99.5955
9	14.	0.2860	99.8815
10	2.	0.0449	99.9265
11	3.	0.0735	100.0000

Total number of input records	48950
Total number of home addresses generated	26628
Total number of accesses	96924
Average number of accesses	1.980

TRIAL NUMBER 3

This trial selects the five high order digits of the remainder after division by 10^6.
    I.D. Number   123456789
    Home Address   45678

TABLE 41. Trial 3 Results

Synonyms	Frequency	Percent	Cumulative Percent
0	1048.	2.1410	2.1410
1	851.	3.4770	5.6180
2	706.	4.3269	9.9448
3	501.	4.0940	14.0388
4	357.	3.6466	17.6854
5	277.	3.3953	21.0807
6	195.	2.7886	23.8693
7	160.	2.6149	26.4842
8	138.	2.5373	29.0214

TABLE 41. Trial 3 Results (continued)

Synonym	Frequency	Percent	Cumulative Percent
9	97.	1.9816	31.0031
10	53.	1.1910	32.1941
11	56.	1.3728	33.5669
12	49.	1.3013	34.8682
13	29.	0.8294	35.6976
14	34.	1.0419	36.7395
15	32.	1.0460	37.7855
16	31.	1.0766	38.8621
17	27.	0.9928	39.8550
18	23.	0.8927	40.7477
19	22.	0.8989	41.6466
20	15.	0.6435	42.2901
21	14.	0.6292	42.9193
22	21.	0.9867	43.9060
23	23.	1.1277	45.0337
24	19.	0.9704	46.0041
25	23.	1.2217	47.2257
26	17.	0.9377	48.1634
27	24.	1.3728	49.5363
28	16.	0.9479	50.4842
29	18.	1.1032	51.5873
30	16.	1.0133	52.6006
31	9.	0.5884	53.1890
32	10.	0.6742	53.8631
33	15.	1.0419	54.9050
34	18.	1.2870	56.1920
35	12.	0.8825	57.0746
36	18.	1.3606	58.4351
37	11.	0.8539	59.2891
38	13.	1.0358	60.3248
39	21.	1.7160	62.0409
40	19.	1.5814	63.6323
41	16.	1.3728	65.0051
42	14.	1.2298	66.2349
43	10.	0.8989	67.1338
44	11.	1.0112	68.1450
45	11.	1.0337	69.1787
46	12.	1.1522	70.3309
47	11.	1.0787	71.4096
48	18.	1.8018	73.2114
49	10.	1.0215	74.2329
50	17.	1.7712	76.0041
51	13.	1.3810	77.3851
52	8.	0.8662	78.2513
53	8.	0.8825	79.1338
54	7.	0.7865	79.9203
55	12.	1.3728	81.2931
56	6.	0.6987	81.9918

TABLE 41. Trial 3 Results (continued)

Synonym	Frequency	Percent	Cumulative Percent
57	12.	1.4219	83.2137
58	13.	1.5669	84.9806
59	5.	0.6129	85.5934
60	9.	1.1216	86.7150
61	9.	1.1399	87.8549
62	5.	0.6435	88.4985
63	8.	1.0460	89.5444
64	4.	0.5312	90.0756
65	4.	0.5393	90.6149
66	1.	0.1369	90.7518
67	2.	0.2778	91.0296
68	4.	0.5638	91.5934
69	1.	0.1430	91.7364
70	5.	0.7252	92.4617
71	4.	0.5884	93.0500
72	2.	0.2983	93.3483
73	3.	0.4535	93.8018
74	4.	0.6129	94.4147
75	4.	0.6210	95.0357
76	3.	0.4719	95.5976
77	1.	0.1593	95.6670
78	0.	0.0000	95.6670
79	0.	0.0000	95.6670
80	2.	0.3309	95.9979
81	4.	0.6701	96.6680
82	2.	0.3391	97.0071
83	0.	0.0000	97.0071
84	3.	0.5209	97.5281
85	1.	0.1757	97.7038
86	1.	0.1777	97.8815
87	0.	0.0000	97.8815
88	0.	0.0000	97.8815
89	3.	0.5516	98.4331
90	0.	0.0000	98.4331
91	0.	0.0000	98.4331
92	1.	0.1900	98.6231
93	1.	0.1920	98.8151
94	2.	0.3882	99.2032
95	0.	0.0000	99.2032
96	2.	0.3963	99.5996
97	2.	0.4004	100.0000

Total number of input records	48950
Total number of home addresses generated	5349
Total number of accesses	809209
Average number of accesses	16.531

Appendix 141

TRIAL NUMBER 4

This trial selects the five high order digits of the remainder after division by 10^7.
I.D. Number 123456789
Home Address 34567

TABLE 42. Trial 4 Results

Synonyms	Frequency	Percent	Cumulative Percent
0	78.	0.5193	0.1593
1	55.	0.2247	0.3841
2	56.	0.2819	0.6660
3	64.	0.5230	1.1890
4	50.	0.5107	1.6997
5	61.	0.7477	2.4474
6	44.	0.6292	3.0766
7	33.	0.5393	3.6159
8	45.	0.8274	4.4433
9	53.	1.0827	5.5260
10	42.	0.9438	6.4699
11	51.	1.2503	7.7201
12	44.	1.1685	8.8887
13	49.	1.4014	10.2901
14	39.	1.1951	11.4852
15	35.	1.1440	12.6292
16	30.	1.0419	13.6711
17	49.	1.8018	15.4729
18	30.	1.1645	16.6374
19	42.	1.7160	18.3534
20	30.	1.2870	19.6404
21	30.	1.4831	21.1236
22	44.	2.0674	23.1910
23	25.	1.2257	24.4168
24	36.	1.8386	26.2554
25	38.	2.0184	28.2737
26	24.	1.3238	29.5975
27	22.	1.2584	30.8560
28	32.	1.8958	32.7518
29	28.	1.7160	34.4678
30	25.	1.5832	36.0511
31	28.	1.8304	37.8815
32	15.	1.0112	38.8927
33	18.	1.2503	40.1430
34	19.	1.3585	41.5015
35	18.	1.3238	42.8253
36	19.	1.4362	44.2615
37	15.	1.1645	45.4259
38	14.	1.1154	46.5414

TABLE 42. Trial 4 Results (continued)

Synonyms	Frequency	Percent	Cumulative Percent
39	17.	1.3892	47.9305
40	16.	1.3401	49.2707
41	15.	1.2870	50.5577
42	19.	1.6691	52.2268
43	13.	1.1685	53.3953
44	9.	0.8274	54.2227
45	11.	1.0337	55.2564
46	6.	0.5761	55.8325
47	12.	1.1767	57.0092
48	9.	0.9009	57.9101
49	13.	1.3279	59.2380
50	10.	1.0419	60.2799
51	5.	0.5312	60.8110
52	5.	0.5414	61.3524
53	6.	0.6619	62.0143
54	9.	1.0112	63.0255
55	5.	0.5720	63.5975
56	8.	0.9316	64.5291
57	8.	0.9479	65.4770
58	13.	1.5669	67.0439
59	2.	0.2451	67.2891
60	6.	0.7477	68.0368
61	7.	0.8866	68.9234
62	4.	0.5148	69.4382
63	3.	0.3922	69.8304
64	7.	0.9295	70.7599
65	4.	0.5393	71.2993
66	10.	1.3687	72.6680
67	4.	0.5557	73.2237
68	5.	0.7048	73.9285
69	4.	0.5720	74.5005
70	2.	0.2901	74.7906
71	5.	0.7354	75.5260
72	3.	0.4474	75.9734
73	5.	0.7559	76.7293
74	5.	0.7661	77.4954
75	4.	0.6210	78.1164
76	8.	1.2584	79.5342
77	1.	0.1593	79.5749
78	6.	0.9683	80.5025
79	1.	0.1634	80.6660
80	6.	0.9928	81.6588
81	3.	0.5026	82.1614
82	2.	0.3391	82.5005
83	3.	0.5148	83.0153
84	2.	0.3473	83.3626
85	1.	0.1757	83.5383
86	1.	0.1777	83.7160

TABLE 42. Trial 4 Results (continued)

Synonyms	Frequency	Percent	Cumulative Percent
87	4.	0.7191	84.4351
88	1.	0.1818	84.6169
89	2.	0.3677	84.9847
90	5.	0.9295	85.9142
91	2.	0.3759	86.2901
92	1.	0.1900	86.4801
93	2.	0.3841	86.8641
94	1.	0.1941	87.0582
95	1.	0.1961	87.2543
96	1.	0.1982	87.4525
97	1.	0.2002	87.6527
98	1.	0.2022	87.8549
99	1.	0.2043	88.0592
100	1.	0.2063	88.2655
101	2.	0.4168	88.6823
102	2.	0.4208	89.1031
103	3.	0.6374	89.7405
104	3.	0.6435	90.3840
105	2.	0.4331	90.8171
106	1.	0.2186	91.0357
107	1.	0.2206	91.2564
108	0.	0.0000	91.2564
109	1.	0.2247	91.4811
110	1.	0.2268	91.7078
111	4.	0.9152	92.6231
112	1.	0.2308	92.8539
113	1.	0.2329	93.0868
114	1.	0.2349	93.3217
115	1.	0.2370	93.5587
116	1.	0.2390	93.7977
117	2.	0.4821	94.2798
118	0.	0.0000	94.2798
119	1.	0.2451	94.5250
120	2.	0.4944	95.0194
121	1.	0.2492	95.2686
122	1.	0.5026	95.7712
123	0.	0.0000	95.7712
124	0.	0.0000	95.7712
125	1.	0.2574	96.0286
126	1.	0.2594	96.2880
127	1.	0.2615	96.5495
128	0.	0.0000	96.5495
129	2.	0.5312	97.0807
130	1.	0.2676	97.3483
131	3.	0.8090	98.1573
132	0.	0.0000	98.1573
133	0.	0.0000	98.1573
134	0.	0.0000	98.1573

TABLE 42. Trial 4 Results (continued)

Synonyms	Frequency	Percent	Cumulative Percent
135	0.	0.0000	98.1573
136	0.	0.0000	98.1573
137	0.	0.0000	98.1573
138	0.	0.0000	98.1573
139	0.	0.0000	98.1573
140	1.	0.2880	98.4453
141	0.	0.0000	98.4453
142	1.	0.2921	98.7374
143	0.	0.0000	98.7374
144	0.	0.0000	98.7374
145	0.	0.0000	98.7374
146	1.	0.3003	99.0378
147	0.	0.0000	99.0378
148	0.	0.0000	99.0378
149	0.	0.0000	99.0378
150	0.	0.0000	99.0378
151	1.	0.3105	99.3483
152	0.	0.0000	99.3483
153	0.	0.0000	99.3483
154	0.	0.0000	99.3483
155	0.	0.0000	99.3483
156	0.	0.0000	99.3483
157	0.	0.0000	99.3483
158	1.	0.3248	99.6731
159	1.	0.3269	100.0000

Total number of input records	48950
Total number of home addresses generated	1818
Total number of accesses	1279445
Average number of accesses	26.138

TRIAL NUMBER 5

This trial selects the five high order digits of the remainder after division by 10^8.
    I.D. Number   123456789
    Home Address   23456

TABLE 43. Trial 5 Results

Synonyms	Frequency	Percent	Cumulative Percent
0	12.	0.0245	0.0245
1	7.	0.0286	0.0531
2	2.	0.0123	0.0654
3	3.	0.0245	0.0899
4	3.	0.0306	0.1205
5	5.	0.0613	0.1818
6	0.	0.0000	0.1818
7	6.	0.0981	0.2799
8	6.	0.1103	0.3902
9	3.	0.0613	0.4515
10	4.	0.0899	0.4904
11	2.	0.0490	0.5904
12	6.	0.1593	0.7497
13	2.	0.0572	0.8069
14	4.	0.1226	0.9295
15	5.	0.1634	1.0930
16	3.	0.1042	1.1971
17	6.	0.2206	1.4178
18	3.	0.1164	1.5342
19	4.	0.1634	1.6977
20	2.	0.0858	1.7835
21	2.	0.0899	1.8733
22	2.	0.0940	1.9673
23	4.	0.1961	2.1634
24	6.	0.3064	2.4699
25	3.	0.1593	2.6292
26	3.	0.1655	2.7947
27	3.	0.1716	2.9663
28	1.	0.0592	3.0255
29	4.	0.2451	3.2707
30	3.	0.1900	3.4607
31	3.	0.1961	3.6568
32	3.	0.2022	3.8590
33	4.	0.2778	4.1369
34	7.	0.5005	4.6374
35	6.	0.4413	5.0787
36	5.	0.3779	5.4566
37	6.	0.4658	5.9224
38	2.	0.1593	6.0817
39	3.	0.2451	6.3269
40	3.	0.2513	6.5781
41	5.	0.4290	7.0071
42	6.	0.5271	7.5342
43	6.	0.5393	8.0735
44	2.	0.1839	8.2574
45	6.	0.5638	8.8212
46	3.	0.2880	9.1093
47	5.	0.4903	9.5996

TABLE 43. Trial 5 Results (continued)

Synonyms	Frequency	Percent	Cumulative Percent
48	5.	0.5005	10.1001
49	1.	0.1021	10.2022
50	3.	0.3126	10.5148
51	3.	0.3187	10.8335
52	3.	0.3248	11.1583
53	3.	0.3309	11.4893
54	4.	0.4494	11.9387
55	3.	0.3432	12.2819
56	2.	0.2329	12.5148
57	2.	0.2370	12.7518
58	6.	0.7232	13.4750
59	7.	0.8580	14.3330
60	3.	0.3739	14.7068
61	2.	0.2533	14.9602
62	5.	0.6435	15.6037
63	5.	0.6537	16.2574
64	8.	1.0623	17.3197
65	4.	0.5393	17.8590
66	1.	0.1369	17.9959
67	2.	0.2778	18.2737
68	2.	0.2819	18.5557
69	8.	1.1440	19.6887
70	1.	0.1450	19.8447
71	4.	0.5884	20.4331
72	6.	0.8948	21.3279
73	3.	0.4535	21.7814
74	4.	0.6129	22.3943
75	5.	0.7763	23.1703
76	5.	0.7865	23.9571
77	6.	0.9561	24.9132
78	5.	0.8069	25.7201
79	4.	0.6537	26.3738
80	0.	0.0000	26.3738
81	1.	0.1675	26.5414
82	4.	0.6782	27.2196
83	2.	0.3432	27.5628
84	3.	0.5209	28.0838
85	4.	0.7028	28.7865
86	4.	0.7109	29.4974
87	4.	0.7191	30.2165
88	2.	0.3636	30.5802
89	3.	0.5516	31.1318
90	1.	0.1859	31.3177
91	3.	0.5638	31.8815
92	1.	0.1900	32.0715
93	2.	0.3841	32.4556
94	3.	0.5822	33.0378
95	4.	0.7845	33.8223

TABLE 43. Trial 5 Results (continued)

Synonyms	Frequency	Percent	Cumulative Percent
96	3.	0.5045	34.4167
97	1.	0.2002	34.6169
98	3.	0.6067	35.2237
99	4.	0.8172	36.0409
100	1.	0.2063	36.2472
101	6.	1.2503	37.4974
102	5.	1.0521	38.5495
103	3.	0.6374	39.1869
104	1.	0.2145	39.4014
105	2.	0.4331	39.8345
106	2.	0.4372	40.2717
107	5.	1.1032	41.3749
108	1.	0.2227	41.5975
109	0.	0.0000	41.5975
110	0.	0.0000	41.5975
111	1.	0.2288	41.8263
112	1.	0.2308	42.0572
113	2.	0.4658	42.5230
114	7.	1.6445	44.1675
115	2.	0.4740	44.6415
116	1.	0.2390	44.8805
117	1.	0.2411	45.1215
118	3.	0.7293	45.8509
119	1.	0.2451	46.0960
120	1.	0.2472	46.3432
121	0.	0.0000	46.3432
122	3.	0.7533	47.0970
123	2.	0.5066	47.6037
124	1.	0.2554	47.8590
125	5.	1.2870	49.1461
126	4.	1.0378	50.1838
127	5.	1.3075	51.4913
128	1.	0.2635	51.7548
129	3.	0.7967	52.5516
130	0.	0.0000	52.5516
131	1.	0.2697	52.8212
132	1.	0.2717	53.0929
133	3.	0.8212	53.9142
134	2.	0.5516	54.4658
135	3.	0.8335	55.2993
136	1.	0.2799	55.5791
137	0.	0.0000	55.5791
138	1.	0.2840	55.8631
139	2.	0.5720	56.4351
140	2.	0.5761	57.0112
141	2.	0.5802	57.5914
142	1.	0.2921	57.8835
143	3.	0.8825	58.7661

Appendix

TABLE 43. Trial 5 Results (continued)

Synonyms	Frequency	Percent	Cumulative Percent
144	1.	0.2962	59.0623
145	0.	0.0000	59.0623
146	3.	0.9009	59.9632
147	1.	0.3023	60.2656
148	1.	0.3044	60.5700
149	5.	1.5322	62.1021
150	1.	0.3085	62.4106
151	1.	0.3105	62.7211
152	0.	0.0000	62.7211
153	2.	0.6292	63.3503
154	2.	0.6333	63.9836
155	0.	0.0000	63.9836
156	3.	0.9622	64.9458
157	1.	0.3228	65.2686
158	1.	0.3248	65.5934
159	2.	0.6537	66.2472
160	1.	0.3289	66.5791
161	2.	0.6619	67.2380
162	1.	0.3330	67.5710
163	2.	0.6701	68.2410
164	1.	0.3371	68.5781
165	0.	0.0000	68.5781
166	1.	0.3412	68.9193
167	0.	0.0000	68.9193
168	2.	0.6905	69.6098
169	2.	0.6946	70.3044
170	0.	0.0000	70.3044
171	2.	0.7028	71.0071
172	1.	0.3534	71.3605
173	0.	0.0000	71.3605
174	0.	0.0000	71.3605
175	1.	0.3596	71.7201
176	0.	0.0000	71.7201
177	2.	0.7273	72.4474
178	2.	0.7314	73.1787
179	2.	0.7354	73.9142
180	1.	0.3698	74.2839
181	0.	0.0000	74.2839
182	0.	0.0000	74.2839
183	1.	0.3759	74.6598
184	1.	0.3779	75.0378
185	0.	0.0000	75.0378
186	0.	0.0000	75.0378
187	1.	0.3841	75.4218
188	2.	0.7722	76.1940
189	2.	0.7763	76.9703
190	1.	0.3902	77.3605
191	0.	0.0000	77.3605

TABLE 43. Trial 5 Results (continued)

Synonyms	Frequency	Percent	Cumulative Percent
192	0.	0.0000	77.3605
193	2.	0.7926	78.1532
194	0.	0.0000	78.1532
195	0.	0.0000	78.1532
196	0.	0.0000	78.1532
197	1.	0.4045	78.5577
198	1.	0.4065	78.9642
199	0.	0.0000	78.9642
200	2.	0.8212	79.7855
OVER 200	38.	20.2145	100.0000

Total number of input records	48950
Total number of home addresses generated	652
Total number of accesses	205021912
Average number of accesses	4198.394

TRIAL NUMBER 6

This trial selects the five high order digits of the characteristic number.
    I.D. Number   123456789
    Home Address   12345

TABLE 44. Trial 6 Results

Synonyms	Frequency	Percent	Cumulative Percent
0	5.	0.0102	0.0102
1	4.	0.0163	0.0266
2	1.	0.0061	0.0327
3	0.	0.0000	0.0327
4	1.	0.0102	0.0429
5	3.	0.0368	0.0797
6	0.	0.0000	0.0797
7	1.	0.0163	0.0960
8	2.	0.0368	0.1328
9	0.	0.0000	0.1328
10	1.	0.0225	0.1553
11	3.	0.0735	0.2288
12	5.	0.1328	0.3616
13	2.	0.0572	0.4188

TABLE 44. Trial 6 Results (continued)

Synonyms	Frequency	Percent	Cumulative Percent
14	2.	0.0613	0.4801
15	3.	0.0981	0.5781
16	2.	0.0695	0.6476
17	2.	0.0735	0.7211
18	1.	0.0388	0.7600
19	4.	0.1634	0.9234
20	1.	0.0429	0.9663
21	2.	0.0899	1.0562
22	2.	0.0940	1.1502
23	3.	0.1471	1.2972
24	3.	0.1532	1.4505
25	1.	0.0531	1.5036
26	2.	0.1103	1.6139
27	3.	0.1716	1.7855
28	2.	0.1185	1.9040
29	4.	0.2451	2.1491
30	2.	0.1267	2.2758
31	3.	0.1961	2.4719
32	3.	0.2022	2.6742
33	1.	0.0695	2.7536
34	4.	0.2860	3.0296
35	5.	0.3677	3.3973
36	5.	0.3779	3.7753
37	2.	0.1553	3.9305
38	4.	0.3187	4.2492
39	3.	0.2451	4.4944
40	1.	0.0838	4.5781
41	4.	0.3432	4.9213
42	7.	0.6149	5.5363
43	4.	0.3596	5.8958
44	0.	0.0000	5.8958
45	3.	0.2819	6.1777
46	5.	0.4801	6.6578
47	1.	0.0981	6.7559
48	6.	0.6006	7.3565
49	1.	0.1021	7.4586
50	2.	0.2084	7.6670
51	3.	0.3187	7.9857
52	2.	0.2165	8.2022
53	3.	0.3309	8.5332
54	4.	0.4494	8.9826
55	2.	0.2288	9.2114
56	1.	0.1164	9.3279
57	2.	0.2370	9.5649
58	5.	0.6027	10.1675
59	4.	0.4903	10.6578
60	2.	0.2492	10.9070
61	1.	0.1267	11.0337

TABLE 44. Trial 6 Results (continued)

Synonyms	Frequency	Percent	Cumulative Percent
62	4.	0.5148	11.5485
63	5.	0.6537	12.2022
64	7.	0.9295	13.1318
65	5.	0.6742	13.8059
66	0.	0.0000	13.8059
67	1.	0.1389	13.9448
68	2.	0.2819	14.2268
69	4.	0.5720	14.7988
70	1.	0.1450	14.9438
71	3.	0.4413	15.3851
72	3.	0.4474	15.8325
73	2.	0.3023	16.1348
74	2.	0.3064	16.4413
75	3.	0.4658	16.9070
76	4.	0.6292	17.5363
77	3.	0.4780	18.0143
78	4.	0.6456	18.6599
79	4.	0.6537	19.3136
80	0.	0.0000	19.3136
81	1.	0.1675	19.4811
82	2.	0.3391	19.8202
83	3.	0.5148	20.3350
84	3.	0.5209	20.8560
85	2.	0.3514	21.2074
86	1.	0.1777	21.3851
87	4.	0.7191	22.1042
88	1.	0.1818	22.2860
89	2.	0.3677	22.6537
90	1.	0.1859	22.8396
91	3.	0.5638	23.4035
92	0.	0.0000	23.4035
93	1.	0.1920	23.5955
94	0.	0.0000	23.5955
95	2.	0.3922	23.9877
96	2.	0.3963	24.3841
97	1.	0.2002	24.5843
98	3.	0.6067	25.1910
99	2.	0.4086	25.5996
100	1.	0.2063	25.8059
101	4.	0.8335	26.6394
102	2.	0.4208	27.0603
103	1.	0.2125	27.2727
104	1.	0.2145	27.4872
105	0.	0.0000	27.4872
106	0.	0.0000	27.4872
107	3.	0.6619	28.1491
108	1.	0.2227	28.3718
109	1.	0.2247	28.3965

TABLE 44. Trial 6 Results (continued)

Synonyms	Frequency	Percent	Cumulative Percent
110	0.	0.0000	28.3965
111	0.	0.0000	28.3965
112	1.	0.2308	28.8274
113	1.	0.2329	29.0603
114	4.	0.9397	30.0000
115	1.	0.2370	30.2370
116	1.	0.2390	30.4760
117	0.	0.0000	30.4760
118	1.	0.2431	30.7191
119	0.	0.0000	30.7191
120	0.	0.0000	30.7191
121	0.	0.0000	30.7191
122	3.	0.7538	31.4729
123	2.	0.5066	31.9796
124	1.	0.2554	32.2349
125	3.	0.7722	33.0071
126	2.	0.5189	33.5260
127	3.	0.7845	34.3105
128	1.	0.2635	34.5740
129	2.	0.5312	35.1052
130	0.	0.0000	35.1052
131	2.	0.5393	35.6445
132	1.	0.2717	35.9162
133	1.	0.2737	36.1900
134	3.	0.8274	37.0174
135	3.	0.8335	37.8509
136	2.	0.5598	38.4106
137	0.	0.0000	38.4106
138	1.	0.2840	38.6946
139	3.	0.8580	39.5526
140	0.	0.0000	39.5526
141	1.	0.2901	39.8427
142	1.	0.2921	40.1348
143	0.	0.0000	40.1348
144	1.	0.2962	40.4310
145	1.	0.2983	40.7293
146	1.	0.3003	41.0296
147	2.	0.6047	41.6343
148	0.	0.0000	41.6343
149	4.	1.2257	42.8601
150	0.	0.0000	42.8601
151	0.	0.0000	42.8601
152	1.	0.3126	43.1726
153	1.	0.3146	43.4872
154	2.	0.6333	44.1205
155	0.	0.0000	44.1205
156	0.	0.0000	44.1205
157	0.	0.0000	44.1205
158	0.	0.0000	44.1205

TABLE 44. Trial 6 Results (continued)

Synonyms	Frequency	Percent	Cumulative Percent
159	0.	0.0000	44.1205
160	0.	0.0000	44.1205
161	1.	0.3309	44.4515
162	1.	0.3330	44.7845
163	1.	0.3350	45.1195
164	1.	0.3371	45.4566
165	0.	0.0000	45.4566
166	1.	0.3412	45.7977
167	0.	0.0000	45.7977
168	1.	0.3453	46.1430
169	2.	0.6946	46.8376
170	0.	0.0000	46.8376
171	0.	0.0000	46.8376
172	2.	0.7068	47.5444
173	1.	0.3555	47.8999
174	0.	0.0000	47.8999
175	1.	0.3596	48.2594
176	0.	0.0000	48.2594
177	1.	0.3636	48.6231
178	1.	0.3657	48.9887
179	0.	0.0000	48.9887
180	1.	0.3698	49.3585
181	0.	0.0000	49.3585
182	0.	0.0000	49.3585
183	0.	0.0000	49.3585
184	0.	0.0000	49.3585
185	0.	0.0000	49.3585
186	0.	0.0000	49.3585
187	0.	0.0000	49.3585
188	3.	1.1583	50.5168
189	1.	0.3882	50.9050
190	2.	0.7804	51.6854
191	0.	0.0000	51.6854
192	1.	0.3943	52.0797
193	1.	0.3963	52.4760
194	1.	0.3984	52.8743
195	0.	0.0000	52.8743
196	0.	0.0000	52.8743
197	1.	0.4045	53.2788
198	1.	0.4065	53.6854
199	0.	0.0000	53.6854
200	2.	0.8212	54.5066
OVER 200	65.	45.4934	100.0000

Total number of input records	48950
Total number of home addresses generated	415
Total number of accesses	548045104
Average number of accesses	9357.408

TRIAL NUMBER 7

This trial selects the five digits remainder after division by the largest prime number under 100,000.

  I.D. Number 123456789
  $$\frac{123456789}{99991} = 1234 \frac{67895}{99991}$$
  Home Address 67895

TABLE 45. Trial 7 Results

Synonyms	Frequency	Percent	Cumulative Percent
2	24075.	49.1828	49.1828
1	8014.	32.7436	81.9265
2	2095.	12.8396	94.7661
3	464.	3.7916	98.5577
4	107.	1.0827	99.6404
5	27.	0.3309	99.9714
6	2.	0.0286	100.0000

Total number of input records	48950
Total number of home addresses generated	34783
Total number of accesses	67540
Average number of accesses	1.380

TRIAL NUMBER 8

This trial selects five of the six low order digits by extraction eliminating the thousands position.

  I.D. Number   123456789
  Home Address   45789

TABLE 46. Trial 8 Results

Synonyms	Frequency	Percent	Cumulative Percent
0	5093.	10.4045	10.4045
1	1891.	7.7263	18.1307
2	1417.	8.6844	26.8151
3	1218.	9.9530	36.7681
4	1089.	11.1236	47.8917
5	924.	11.3258	59.2176
6	719.	10.2819	69.4995
7	537.	8.7763	78.2758

TABLE 46. Trial 8 Results (continued)

Synonyms	Frequency	Percent	Cumulative Percent
8	412.	7.5751	85.8509
9	246.	5.0255	90.8764
10	158.	3.5506	94.4270
11	97.	2.3779	06.8049
12	59.	1.5669	98.3718
13	30.	0.8580	99.2298
14	16.	0.4903	99.7201
15	4.	0.1307	99.8509
16	2.	0.0695	99.9203
17	0.	0.0000	99.9203
18	1.	0.0388	99.9591
19	1.	0.0409	100.0000

Total number of input records	48950
Total number of home addresses generated	13914
Total number of accesses	168404
Average number of accesses	3.440

TRIAL NUMBER 9

This trial selects five of the digits extracting the two low order digits of sub-field one and the three low order digits of sub-field two.

I.D. Number	123456789
Home Address	34789

TABLE 47. Trial 9 Results

Synonyms	Frequency	Percent	Cumulative Percent
0	25562.	52.2206	52.2206
1	7361.	30.0756	82.2962
2	1822.	11.1665	93.4627
3	512.	4.1839	97.6466
4	151.	1.5424	99.1890
5	46.	0.5638	99.7528
6	15.	0.2145	99.9673
7	2.	0.0327	100.0000

Total number of input records	48950
Total number of home addresses generated	35471
Total number of accesses	67420
Average number of accesses	1.377

156   Appendix

TRIAL NUMBER 10

This trial selects the five middle digits of the square of the home address as derived in trial number 8.

I.D. Number	123456789
Extraction	45789
Squared	2096632521
Home Address	66325

TABLE 48. Trial 10 Results

Synonyms	Frequency	Percent	Cumulative Percent
0	4395.	8.9785	8.9785
1	1762.	7.1992	16.1777
2	1314.	8.0531	24.2308
3	1134.	9.2666	33.4974
4	1025.	10.4699	43.9673
5	892.	10.9336	54.9009
6	672.	9.9608	64.5107
7	532.	8.6946	73.2053
8	387.	7.1154	80.3207
9	250.	5.1073	85.4280
10	159.	3.5730	89.0010
11	113.	2.7702	91.7712
12	65.	1.7263	93.4974
13	49.	1.4014	94.8989
14	34.	1.0419	95.9408
15	16.	0.5230	96.4637
16	10.	0.3473	96.8110
17	8.	0.2942	97.1052
18	12.	0.4658	97.5710
19	12.	0.4903	98.0613
20	1.	0.0429	98.1042
21	4.	0.1798	98.2840
22	3.	0.1410	98.4249
23	1.	0.0490	98.4739
24	4.	0.2043	98.6782
25	4.	0.2125	98.8907
26	1.	0.0552	98.9459
27	2.	0.1144	99.0603
28	1.	0.0592	99.1195
29	1.	0.0613	99.1808
30	1.	0.0633	99.2441
31	2.	0.1307	99.3749
32	0.	0.0000	99.3749
33	0.	0.0000	99.3749
34	0.	0.0000	99.3749
35	0.	0.0000	99.3749
36	0.	0.0000	99.3749
37	0.	0.0000	99.3749

TABLE 48. Trial 10 Results (continued)

Synonyms	Frequency	Percent	Cumulative Percent
38	0.	0.0000	99.3749
39	1.	0.0817	99.4566
40	0.	0.0000	99.4566
41	1.	0.0858	99.5424
42	0.	0.0000	99.5424
43	0.	0.0000	99.5424
44	1.	0.0919	99.6343
45	0.	0.0000	99.6343
46	0.	0.0000	99.6343
47	1.	0.0981	99.7324
48	1.	0.1001	99.8325
49	0.	0.0000	99.8325
50	0.	0.0000	99.8325
51	0.	0.0000	99.8325
52	0.	0.0000	99.8325
53	0.	0.0000	99.8325
54	0.	0.0000	99.8325
55	0.	0.0000	99.8325
56	0.	0.0000	99.8325
57	0.	0.0000	99.8325
58	0.	0.0000	99.8325
59	0.	0.0000	99.8325
60	0.	0.0000	99.8325
61	0.	0.0000	99.8325
62	0.	0.0000	99.8325
63	0.	0.0000	99.8325
64	0.	0.0000	99.8325
65	0.	0.0000	99.8325
66	0.	0.0000	99.8325
67	0.	0.0000	99.8325
68	0.	0.0000	99.8325
69	0.	0.0000	99.8325
70	0.	0.0000	99.8325
71	0.	0.0000	99.8325
72	0.	0.0000	99.8325
73	0.	0.0000	99.8325
74	0.	0.0000	99.8325
75	0.	0.0000	99.8325
76	0.	0.0000	99.8325
77	0.	0.0000	99.8325
78	0.	0.0000	99.8325
79	0.	0.0000	99.8325
80	0.	0.0000	99.8325
81	1.	0.1675	100.0000

Total number of input records	48950
Total number of home addresses generated	12872
Total number of accesses	193746
Average number of accesses	3.958

Index

Access, 38, 41, 43, 44, 61, 91, 102, 117
Address, 12, 28, 29, 36, 44, 45, 54-55
Algorithm, 18, 26, 28, 39, 42-43, 47, 128
Alphanumeric, 21
Associative memory, 26, 28
Autocoder, 49
Automated information system, 86
Automation, 4

BAL, 49
Batch, 17
BEST, 21
Bit, 6
Bit indicators, 100-101

Category linkage, 57, 61, 63-65, 67, 68, 88, 89, 90, 92, 93, 94, 95, 124
Chain, 26-28, 62
Chaining, 36, 48
Chaining address, 48
Chain link, 26, 68
Check character, 48, 50, 54, 55, 90, 93, 94, 95, 124
Closed loop, 98
COBOL, 21, 49
Completeness, 25-26
Control number, 18
Control record, 58-59, 62, 65
Control system, 3, 4, 20, 26
Corporate policy, 3
Cost, 12, 17, 46, 67
Cost-Benefit, 1
Cylinder, 10, 31, 32-35, 49, 81
Cylinder index, 32

Data bank, 22-23
Data entry, 54
Data management, 123, 125

Data organization, 11
Data processing, 23, 25
Data retrieval and storage, 16
Data track, 11
Debug, 126
Descriptors, 19
Direct access, 8
Directory, 18
Disk pack, 7-10
Disk processing, 98-99, 102, 123, 126
Disk records, 55
Disk storage, 15

EDP, 2
Education, 12-13, 15, 40-41
Educational administration, 87-92, 125
Efficiency, 26, 81, 98
Elapsed time, 13
End linking, 26-28
End-of-chain sentinel, 29
Engineering, 1
Entry, 2, 6, 28, 38-39, 44
Evaluation, 40-41
Evaluator, 40
Evolutionary approach, 20
Extracting, 37,

Facility category, 63-64, 67
Facility chain, 63
Field code, 21
File creation, 39, 55
File design, 15
File maintenance, 59, 82-85
File organization, 21, 25-26
Flexibility, 20
Flow, 5
Flow chart, 39, 128
Food and Drug Administration, 97

159

Index

FORTRAN, 49
Frequency, 80, 81, 82
Frequency of occurrence, 82

GE 9PAC, 21
GE 225, 20
General activity, 16
General Electric, 20-21
Generalized information system, 19-20, 21
Government, 20, 25

Hardware, 1, 2, 5, 26
Hollerith, 5
Horizontal, 31
Hospital administration, 92-98, 125
Hospitals, 23-25

IBM, 21, 22, 39
IBM GIS, 18-19
IBM KWIC system, 19
IBM 305 RAMAC, 22
IBM 360, Model 40, 54
IBM 709, 21
IBM 1301, 39
IBM 1405 disk storage, 18
IBM 2311 disk storage, 8, 54
IBM 7044, 39-40, 43, 46
Identification, 48, 55, 81, 101, 124
Index, 19
   sequential, 28, 31, 32, 35, 38, 127
Indexing, 18, 28-30, 38, 39
Information explosion, 1, 3, 123
Information files, 1, 17, 127
Information processing, 1
Information retrieval, 12, 23
Information system, 4, 123
Input/Output, 9
Inquiry, 83
Integrated data store, 21
Integrated file, 25
Internal linkage, 48, 69, 124
Interrelate, 16
Iowa Education Information Center, 22, 39
Iowa Test of Basic Skills, 39
Iowa Test of Education Development, 39

Key-word-in-context, 19
Key words, 12

Legal profession, 25

Libraries, 12
Linear programming, 64-65
Linkage, 2, 23, 26, 48-50, 55, 56, 60, 86, 124, 127
Linking, 15, 55
Logical file, 17-18, 21, 24
Logical linkage, 21, 80
Logical record, 16

Magnetic tape, 6-7, 87, 99
Maintenance, 54, 59, 80, 82, 128
Management, 1, 3-5, 15, 19, 86, 123
Management information, 3, 86
Management information system, 1, 3-4, 15, 16, 98
Management Operating System (MOS), 22
Master, 17, 20, 100, 122
Medical, 23, 24
Memory, 5, 100
Memory address, 18
Monitor control, 20
Multiple category, 68
Multiple level, 68

National Cash Register, 21

Occurrence, 80, 82
Off line, 99
On line, 7, 17, 90, 96, 99
Operational control, 23, 25
Organizations, 1, 2
Overflow, 28, 29, 36, 49, 50, 55, 56, 88, 89, 90, 93, 94, 95, 124, 127

Parallel processing, 102
Probabilistic, 102
Product distribution, 15
Product information, 50, 53-54, 55
Production, 14
Production facility information, 50, 52, 53-54, 55
Programmers, 1, 42
Programming, 2, 11, 20, 43, 46, 85, 86
Project Talent, 22
Punched card, 5-6, 99

Random access, 8, 11-12, 15, 17, 35, 49, 58, 59, 86, 98-99
Random file, 12, 18

Index

Random processing, 12, 17, 36, 123-124, 127
Randomizer, 39, 40-41, 46, 47, 135-157
Randomizing, 28-29, 36, 38-39, 40, 42,
    45, 46, 48, 81, 97, 102
  algorithm, 38, 39, 47, 135
Read-write head, 7, 10, 31, 32
Real time, 20, 23, 85
Record identification, 48
Record length, 49
Record placement, 80-82
Relevance, 25-26
Remote consoles, 86
Response, 25, 86
Retrieval, 12, 16, 31, 38, 85-86, 91, 127
Retrieval language, 85

Salesman information, 50, 53-54, 55
Searching, 25-26
Segregated activity, 17
Sequential entry, 28, 31-36
Sequential file, 6, 13, 18, 124
Sequential processing, 1-2, 6, 7, 12-15, 17,
    36, 123-124, 127
Software, 5, 19, 22, 35, 47
Squaring, 37
Storage, 1, 11, 16
  capacity, 8
Structured information files, 2, 12, 14, 15,
    16, 50, 53, 55, 58-59, 60, 62, 65,

Structured information files *(continued)*
    69, 80, 86, 91, 92, 96, 98, 123,
    125, 126, 128
Sub-field, 56-57, 61, 63, 124
Surface index, 32, 35
Synonym, 18, 50, 54, 55, 80-82, 88, 89,
    90, 93, 94, 95, 124
System analysis, 1, 2, 42, 47
System design, 42, 86, 125, 126
System Development Corporation, 24
System response, 25-26

Tape files, 90, 98-100
Tape processing, 98-102, 126
Technology, 2, 3
Timeliness, 25-26
Total information system, 123
Truncating, 37

Univac Fastrand, 24
Unstructured file, 12, 13, 15
Up-dating, 2, 17, 18, 82, 127

Validity, 2
Vertical, 31

Warehouse Information, 50, 52, 53-54, 55
World War II, 3

QA
76.6
K34

JAN 20 1975